Cooking on the Go

COOKING ON THE GO

Revised Edition

Janet Groene

Hearst Marine Books
New York

Library of Congress Cataloging-in-Publication Data

Groene, Janet.
  Cooking on the go.

  Originally published: Boston : Sail Books, c 1980.
  Includes index.

  1. Outdoor cookery.   2. Cookery, Marine.   I. Title.
  [TX823.G76   1987]   641.5'75   86-33500
  ISBN 0-688-07200-3 (pbk.)

Printed in the United States of America

FIRST REVISED EDITION

1 2 3 4 5 6 7 8 9 10

To M. who made me love cooking; to D. who made me love cooking in galley and camp; to G. who made me love cooking in galley and camp for him.

CONTENTS

Part III   SPECIAL SITUATIONS

Part IV   PROVISIONING

Part I

TECHNIQUES

1. HOW TO USE THIS BOOK

It is the promise of *Cooking on the Go* that there will be no unpleasant surprises for the galley cook who has no oven or refrigeration. So often, boating recipes begin with canned chicken but go on to demand cream cheese, frozen broccoli, or a broiled topping. The recipes here, however, depend entirely on ingredients which can be carried aboard for weeks and even months. Look over the recipes before you sail, to help plan your provisioning and shopping lists. If you find an ingredient that you don't know how to provide months away from port, consult the Glossary, which will tell you how to preserve or where to buy the ingredient. Cheeses, for example, are almost always kept in refrigerators at home. Yet cheese has been around centuries longer than refrigeration has. Today you can buy cheese in many forms, including freeze-dried cottage cheese and cheddar in cans.

Every recipe and ingredient in this book was included for a reason, even though each may not suit your own galley, taste, or boating situation. Except for special chapters in Part III, my recipes require no freshly purchased foods, no oven, and no waste of precious water. Where you encounter ingredients which you think can't be carried because you have no refrigerator or freezer aboard, check the Glossary to learn how you can enjoy these foods when you're far from port. At the end of the Glossary, there is also a list of mail order sources for some of the lesser-known items, such as enameled tins for long-term stowage and smoked hams which require no refrigeration. When my cooking directions call for baking, I'm referring to baking atop the stove as described in Chapter 2.

Just as ingredients and recipes were chosen for good reason, others were omitted for a reason. I assume that you'll also have a good, basic cookbook such as *Joy of Cooking.* It is not my aim here to cover such cooking fundamentals as how to make a white sauce, cut fat into dry ingredients, or hard-boil an egg. A comprehensive, general cookbook will cover these subjects and will include whatever recipes are necessary for fresh foods when you can get them.

I have also not tried to cover all the exotic cooking styles and ingredients you'll find in various cruising areas. Entire and excellent books have been written on Caribbean cooking, Mediterranean specialties, Oriental favorites, vegetarian meals, microwaving, living off the sea, and other cooking which may apply to the kind of cruise you are planning. If you find that you like sprouting and the taste of the many types of sprouts which can be kept aboard, you may want to get a sprouts cookbook. If you eat a lot of fish aboard, get a fish cookbook. I've tried not to overemphasize any one type of cooking or provisioning.

The reader with some home economics background may find many of my recipes frustratingly inexact, but I've found that very few recipes are exact chemical equations and few will be ruined by a little fiddling and substituting. Some of the best dishes I've ever cooked aboard resulted from desperate gambles that one herb would be better than another or that candied cherries would work when I was out of raisins.

Those of you who have fully equipped galleys, complete with microwave oven and freezer, may ask what use this book can be to you. My answer is, perhaps none—until the day it's so hot you don't want to use the oven; the day the generator or freezer fails, leaving you with only canned and packaged goods; the time when fuel is running low and you don't dare use the oven; or the next trip when you want to eat out of your stored foods for days at a time.

1. HOW TO USE THIS BOOK

All of us need stowed foods at some time. Sailors and campers have used *Cooking on the Go* since the first edition appeared in the 1970s. Homebodies have used it to create an emergency shelf of stores that can be used for anything from hurricanes to truck strikes. College students like this book because they can create most of the recipes with one hot plate and little other equipment.

Shut-ins use it when they can't get to the supermarket. It can be your guide for provisioning a condo at the beach for a week, or a cabin in Alaska for a long winter. If you pack supplies into a hunting lodge only once a year, let this book help you plan supplies and recipes to utilize them. If you're going on a long RV ramble in Baja, or want to buy supplies in the lower forty-eight to avoid paying high prices in Alaska, these provisioning lists can help.

If you need any help with galley problems, or have hints to offer, please write me % Hearst Marine Books, 105 Madison Avenue, New York, N.Y. 10016.

—JANET GROENE

13

2. WHEN RECIPES CALL FOR BAKING

Even though you have no oven aboard there are four basic ways you can make the baked recipes in this book:

Pressure cooker direct. The heavier your pressure cooker, the more successful this baking will be. Older cookers are thicker than new; aluminum cookers spread heat better than stainless steel. Grease the cooker heavily, sprinkle with cornmeal, and shake so the coating is even. Then add the bread dough for its final raising. If you are baking a sweet dough or cake batter, omit the cornmeal. If you are baking a non-yeast dough, you will, of course, omit the final rising step. Place the lid on the pressure cooker and bake without the pressure regulator, letting steam escape, over a low-medium flame. Depending on the type and controllability of your stove, you may need a flame shield. Some are metal, some are asbestos, but you can find such flame tamers in housewares and gourmet stores. My asbestos flame shield was bought in a dime store for less than two dollars.

A loaf of bread which takes four cups of flour bakes in my heavy, four-quart pressure cooker in 45 minutes atop a shielded, kerosene Primus burner. Some cooks turn over the loaf halfway through the cooking time for more even browning, but I prefer to leave the top white rather than risk burns or a fallen loaf.

Pressure cooker indirect. Here, your pressure cooker serves as a separate oven. Place the rack in the bottom of the cooker and make sure to remove the pressure relief valve and the rubber ring because they are damaged by high heat. Put the dough into any pan that fits inside the pressure cooker (with the rack in place). Greased tin cans are ideal because they are tall and thin and produce pretty little round loaves or cakes. This method is best for firm cakes and for quick breads. Yeast loaves may not brown well. Preheat the cooker for about ten minutes over high heat. Take off the lid, quickly place the baking pan(s) inside, and replace the lid. Don't peek until the baking time is almost up. Do not raise pressure.

Dutch oven direct. If you have a heavy, well-lidded skillet, Dutch oven, or roasting pan, you can bake bread, pastries, or meat loaf directly in the greased pan atop the galley stove. Cornbread and other quick breads are traditionally baked this way at home, but I've used this method, too, for layer cakes, Yorkshire pudding, and other foods you think of as oven products. Start with a cold pan, grease it thoroughly, and add the batter, pizza, meatloaf and baking potatoes, or dough. Place the lidded pan over a low-medium flame with shield. Aluminum, the thicker the better, is best over burners. Iron pans work better on wood, diesel, or charcoal stoves where the heat is distributed evenly over the entire underside of the pan. Over burners, iron skillets develop hot spots. Stainless steel, which does not season as iron and aluminum do, is the poorest choice of all for stovetop baking.

Dutch oven indirect. Start with a clean skillet, roaster, or Dutch oven which has no grease anywhere. Any stains will bake on so the pan should be immaculate. Preheat the oven/skillet for about ten minutes. During preheating the oven should be tightly lidded so heat is transferred evenly to bottom, sides and cover. Put batter, casserole, or dough in a pan, place the baking pan on a rack inside the oven, and bake with minimal peeking until the product tests done. This, too, is best for quick breads and cakes. Yeast doughs do not brown well in the moist heat. Browning will be better if the dough or pastry is made with margarine rather than shortening.

Other bread methods. In addition to these "oven" methods, there are other ways to cast your bread upon the waters. English

muffins have always been baked on a griddle, and biscuits can be baked in a covered, heavy skillet. Turn either of these carefully so rising is not interrupted. Many traditional ethnic breads, such as chappatis and tortillas, are skillet-baked. Others, like Swedish rye, are steamed. Cornmeal dough, when deep-fried in hot fat, becomes hush puppies. Yeast doughs are delicious deep-fried, too.

About folding campstove ovens. Stovetop camp ovens are preferred by some galley cooks. If you decide to buy one, get a folding type that won't be a stowage problem, and opt for the costly all–stainless steel type to guard against rust. While camp ovens do cook with a drier heat than the other types of stovetop ovens I've described, they are hard to keep up to baking temperature. If your fuel is alcohol or if there is any breeze in the galley, it's almost impossible to keep these thin ovens at 350° F. They radiate heat quickly so they are unpleasant to use in hot weather, and they are tippy and top-heavy underway.

What about oven temperatures? Most home baking is done at temperatures between 325° and 450° F., with 350° considered a "moderate" oven. In my stovetop baking, I don't make any attempt to take thermometer readings yet I always get a good result, without burning or the cake falling. Much of this is based on practice, and you'll very soon get the hang of baking without a thermostat. Some of it may be luck, and much of the success is, I believe, because most recipes can take a lot more inexactness than some writers indicate.

In general, all indirect baking should be done at the highest flame your stove has. You may find that, if yours is a very hot flame, you can turn down the fire after beginning to bake, but do preheat the Dutch oven or pressure cooker at the higher temperature.

Direct baking requires more caution, and times and temperatures will vary greatly according to the type of fuel you use and the effectiveness of your burner. Buy one or two flame shields, and you'll soon know what is needed with your particular galley stove. Gas, kerosene, and alcohol stoves are easier to regulate; electric burners are more difficult to control when you want an even, average heat for direct baking.

Don't be afraid to try, guess, improvise, and take chances. You'll be amazed at how easy stovetop baking can be.

3. PRESSURE COOKING

Pressure cookers cook foods faster than saucepans do and, in many cases, even faster than microwave ovens. This speed is especially important to the galley cook because it means a savings not just of time but of fuel. Because the lid locks on, this is the safest pot you can use underway, even when you are not raising pressure. And because cooking times are reduced and your cooking flame is turned off sooner, the danger of a galley fire is reduced. In addition, the pressure cooker serves as a saucepan, oven, canner, Dutch oven, and steamer all in one.

Despite its many talents, I'm surprised to find that so many galley cooks fear the pressure cooker because they heard of someone's Aunt Hattie who had applesauce explode over her farmhouse ceiling. Pressure cookers are better than ever, thanks to new designs and know-how. Modern instruction books tell you clearly what to do and what not to do, and the new Presto safety valves fit older cookers.

Shop flea markets and thrift shops for the oldest aluminum cooker you can find. The heavier-gauge metals used in older cookers are best for stovetop baking, and I specify aluminum because it's a better baker than stainless steel is. I'm still able to buy gaskets for my 25-year-old Presto cooker, and I recommend that brand because you're not always able to get parts for other older cookers.

My own pressure cooker is a four-quart size but if your crew is more numerous you may want the six-quart. Larger cookers, and the big pressure canners, are too unwieldy for all but the bigger boats. If you buy a used cooker and have no instruction book, write the manufacturer and ask for one because it's important that you follow directions precisely. They vary from model to model, according to the type of pressure regulator used, but some general precautions can be mentioned here. One is to fill the cooker no more than two-thirds full, being especially conservative when you're cooking a foamy food such as applesauce or dried beans. Another is to avoid removing the pressure regulator or the lid while any pressure remains in the pan. One sailor told me his regulator flew off during a knockdown so it's best to avoid pressure cooking in the scrappiest seas. Pot clamps and a gimballed stove should solve most problems when you're cooking underway.

Besides earlier accidents, pressure cookers have taken a bad rap because so many cooks pressure everything too long and ruin delicate foods such as fish or asparagus. Two innovative new pressure cooker cookbooks have appeared, and I recommend them. One is Roy Andries De Groot's *Pressure Cookery Perfected* from Summit Books. De Groot is a gourmet cook whose pressure cooker recipes accent shorter cooking times and coddling of flavors. Another book is *Pressure Cooking is Pleasure Cooking*, published by Presto Industries in Eau Claire WI 54701. This book has lots of recipes, including some for complete meals with desserts that can be cooked all at once.

If your pressure cooker has just one weight, with no choice of 5, 10, or 15 pounds, you may be able to order other weights from the manufacturer. I'd also suggest that you write to Presto Industries, Eau Claire WI 54701, for new canning instructions at 15 pounds pressure. Older canning books sometimes called for five or ten pounds but a method has been developed for canning at 15 pounds for shorter times.

For information about using your pressure cooker as an oven, see page 15.

Although my enthusiasm for pressure cookers is unreserved, there is one warning for galley cooks. A number of cruising books and magazine articles recommend a method which is said to "can" food for several days. The technique involves making a big batch of stew or other one-dish meal. You eat what you want the first day, bring the pot up to pressure again, let it stand, repeat the heat–eat process on the third day, and so on.

This is both mechanically and microbiologically unsound. First, the cooled cooker has no vacuum to "can" foods. Air reenters the cooker as it cools, through the same passages where air exits during heating. Second, the growth of harmful organisms can continue in a warm, moist atmosphere, and food poisoning is a very real possibillty. Although the idea of such pressure-cooker canning is based on a process known as Tyndalization, in which foods are heated repeatedly, the game is too chancy for the galley. I believe that many cases of "seasickness" in the first few days of a long passage are caused by food poisoning through the popular use of this trick.

Part II

COOKING WITH NO OVEN OR REFRIGERATION

4. BREAKFASTS

 ## Idiot-Proof Kuchen

Over the years, batch after batch of this buttery, flaky, can't-fail coffee cake has been baked in my galley over the Primus burner. Its best feature is that you don't have to watch it, as you do many yeast doughs, to double in bulk. Make it the night before and bake it in the morning.

½ cup milk
1 package yeast (1 tablespoon)
2 cups flour
1 tablespoon sugar
1 teaspoon salt
½ cup butter or margarine
1 or 2 eggs

If you are using fresh milk, scald it and let it cool. There is no need to scald reconstituted dry or canned milk when using yeast. Warm the milk, sprinkle in yeast, and let stand for a minute or two. Then stir egg(s) into milk. Cut the fat into the dry ingredients and stir in milk mixture. Spread the dough in a cake or pie pan, sprinkle with cinnamon sugar, and top with nuts, sliced apples, or your favorite coffee-cake topping. Cover lightly with a linen towel or plastic wrap, and let stand several hours or overnight. Bake according to indirect Dutch oven method over high heat until brown and flaky, or about 30 to 45 minutes.

Quicky Sticky Buns

Melt three tablespoons butter in a roomy skillet and add your own biscuits (see page 218) by the heaping teaspoonful. Bake, covered, on both sides a total of about 12 minutes or until the biscuits are browned and done through. Add a quarter-cup honey or maple syrup and a quarter-cup of finely chopped nuts. Then toss, turning the biscuits over and over, using a low flame, until they are well coated.

See page 219 for a master-mix recipe for pancakes. To vary this, add the following pancake recipes to your menus.

Orange Pancakes

1½ cups self-rising flour or 1½ cups flour, 2 teaspoons
     baking powder, and ½ teaspoon salt
1 teaspoon sugar
2 eggs
½ cup milk
½ cup orange juice or orange drink
3 tablespoons salad oil
16-ounce can cream-style corn

Put the dry ingredients in a large bowl and mix with a balloon whisk. Add the remaining ingredients and whisk until well blended. Using a quarter-cup measure for each pancake, bake on a preheated, lightly greased griddle until bubbles form on top, then flip over and cook until the other side browns. This recipe makes about 16 big four-inch pancakes. Serve with your favorite syrup or:

Apricot-Rum Syrup

1½ tablespoons cornstarch
2 tablespoons water or juice
1½ cups apricot nectar
1 cup sugar
½ cup rum
1 large can, or 2 small cans, mandarin oranges, drained

In a paper cup, blend the cornstarch with the two table-spoons water or liquid from the canned oranges. Combine the remaining ingredients except for the oranges in a saucepan. Add the cornstarch mixture and heat, stirring, until it's smooth and thickened. Fold in the mandarin oranges. Serve over pancakes or crepes. Leftover syrup is good with pudding or pound cake.

Cinnamon Cream Syrup

1 cup sugar
½ cup light corn syrup
¼ cup water
½ teaspoon cinnamon
½ cup evaporated milk

Bring everything but the milk to a boil, stirring constantly, and remove from heat. Cool several minutes before stirring in milk. Serve at once. It's delicious with apple pancakes.

Mapley Syrup

When you are provisioning for a very long time, it takes less space to carry sugar and maple flavoring than to stock bottle after bottle of pancake syrup. If you are pancake eaters, take maple flavor because both the flavoring and the syrup are rare outside North America. It costs less to make your own, too. This syrup keeps several weeks without refrigeration. If you use syrup rarely, make half a recipe. This recipe makes enough to fill one Squeeze Parkay bottle—an excellent, drip-free way to carry syrup.

2 cups sugar
1 cup water
½ teaspoon imitation maple flavoring
a few drops of imitation vanilla-butter flavoring (optional)

Bring the sugar and water to a boil. Remove from heat and stir in the flavorings. It's best if you cool it to lukewarm before serving.

Jelly Doughnuts

This is a very good way to use up stale bread. It works best with square sandwich bread with crusts cut off, but any bread will do.

bread, jelly, and fat for deep frying
1½ cups biscuit mix
1 tablespoon sugar
1 teaspoon baking powder
1 egg
¾ cup milk
a dash of cinnamon
granulated or confectioners' sugar

Use the bread and jelly to make sandwiches, then cut each sandwich into three or four "fingers." In a flat-bottom bowl, make a batter by whisking together the biscuit mix, baking powder, milk, sugar, cinnamon, and egg. Heat about an inch of oil in a skillet or roomy saucepan until it will brown a cube of bread in 50 seconds (370°). Dip each sandwich finger into the batter, then deep-fry until golden. Roll in sugar if you like.

Skillet Peach Cobbler

Ann Glenn, cooking for her guests aboard the charter tri-maran *Encore* out of St. Thomas, also serves this cobbler with whipped cream for dessert. It's a quick, hot, one-pot stovetop breakfast.

1 large can (29 ounces) sliced peaches, undrained
4 tablespoons brown sugar, reserve 1 tablespoon
2 tablespoons butter
a dash of salt
½ teaspoon ginger (or cinnamon)
3 tablespoons cornstarch
1 cup buttermilk biscuit mix
⅓ cup milk

Put the peaches, brown sugar, butter, salt, and spice into a skillet or saucepan. Make a smooth paste with the peach liquid and the cornstarch, then add it to the first mixture. In a bowl, briefly blend the baking mix, milk, and the reserved tablespoon of brown sugar just until mixed. Bring the peach mixture to the boil until it is clear and thick, then drop the dumplings by table-spoonsful into the boiling liquid. Cook uncovered ten minutes, then cover and cook ten minutes more. Serve with sausage, bacon, or canned ham.

Bread and Applesauce

This is a family tradition, served by Lee and Phyllis Bowring aboard their charter boat *Sea Demon* out of St. Thomas. It is easy, and deliciously unusual because of the blend of flavors. It elimi-nates the need to make endless pieces of toast at the last minute, and it can be prepared ahead of time to assemble as various crew members come to the table. Quantities vary according to appe-tites.

Butter slices of bread generously and place on plates. Top each with two or three slices of crisply fried bacon. Just before serving, ladle the bread generously with hot applesauce. This melts the butter to combine tastily with the applesauce and bread, and the bacon provides crunchy texture contrast.

🍂 Breakfast Fritters

Begin with a scant cup of biscuit mix per person. Add enough milk, plus an egg if you like, to make a stiff dough. Fold in cut-up, well-drained canned fruit, not more than a quarter-cup per cup of biscuit mix. Drop by heaping teaspoonsful into hot oil as described above. Fry until golden and drain on absorbent paper. Serve sprinkled with confectioners' sugar, shake in a bag with cinnamon sugar, or serve in bowls with syrup. You can also make fruitier fritters with large hunks of fruit. Start with a cup of biscuit mix and add milk until it's the thickness of heavy cream. Dip large, well-drained pieces of fruit such as apple, pineapple, or peach into the batter to coat them. Then deep-fry as described above.

🍩 Fried Dough

Early in the day, make a double batch of your favorite bread recipe and save half to bake as a loaf. Use the other half, after the first rising, to make doughnuts. Simply tear off walnut-size bits of dough, arrange them on a plate in a warm place to rise, then deep-fry them until golden. Drain on paper toweling, then shake them in a bag with confectioners' sugar, granulated sugar, or cinnamon sugar.

Variation: let the dough rise once, then pinch off chunks the size of a small tangerine. Roll each into a circle large enough to wrap a peeled, hard-boiled egg. Pinch the edges well to seal in the egg and then deep-fry until golden.

Jury-Rig Eggs Benedict

First, prepare a package of hollandaise sauce mix according to directions. Make a stack with a piece of toast or half a toasted English muffin, ham, a few spears of asparagus if you like, and top with a poached egg. Lavish with hollandaise. Work note: I make the hollandaise first and keep it warm in a heavy, lidded pan or in a thermos bottle. Then I make the toast and top with unheated ham and asparagus. It's then easy to create a hot dish by adding poached egg and sauce just before serving.

 ## Mock Hollandaise #1

You can put together a quick mock hollandaise as follows:

1 cup mayonnaise or salad dressing (1 eight-ounce jar)
½ cup yogurt
1 teaspoon mustard
1½ tablespoons lemon juice

Whisk together over very low heat until just heated through. Do not boil. Cover and set aside, and whisk again before serving.

Mock Hollandaise #2

Here's another version. Make one recipe of medium white sauce (see page 61). When it is completed, remove from heat and stir a little of the hot sauce into two egg yolks, then add the egg mixture to the sauce. Add two tablespoons lemon juice and stir.

A Craving for Crepes

Although crepes are made tediously, one at a time, they are one of the most versatile treats you can make for breakfast, brunch, lunch, or dinner. For a morning meal, wrap hot crepes around scrambled eggs or a ripe banana. For a more substantial breakfast, fill yours with a creamed mixture containing mushrooms and ham, crab, or vegetables. Wrapped around a mixture of cottage cheese and raw egg and fried in butter until the filling sets, crepes become blintzes. Filled with meat and vegetables and deep-fried, they are Chinese egg rolls. Sautéed and flamed, they become Crepes Suzette.

2 eggs
1 cup flour
2 teaspoons cornstarch
½ teaspoon salt
2 cups water

Whisk all ingredients together until smooth. The batter will be very thin. Heat and very lightly oil a skillet which is about six inches in diameter. I have used both enameled steel and T-Fal skillets with good results, but do not overheat T-Fal. The object is to make a very thin pancake by putting a small amount of batter into the pan. Quickly tip the pan until it is coated with the mixture. However, if you add batter after cooking has started, to fill a gap, the crepe will have a seam which may break when you are filling it. So experiment with a quarter-cup measure until you know how much batter it takes to make a crepe of the right thickness in your pan. After the crepe bakes on one side (use a medium flame), brown the other side lightly. Stack between paper toweling or clean linen dish towels.

Fill with:

🐚 Crepe Filling #1

1 can cream of mushroom soup
2 tablespoons mayonnaise, sour cream, or yogurt
1 small can mushrooms, drained
1 small can baby peas, drained
¾ cup grated cheese such as cheddar
1 small can Tender Chunk ham, shredded

Combine the soup and mayonnaise (or substitute) in a saucepan over low heat and whisk until smooth. Add the remaining ingredients and heat gently until heated through. Divide among 12 crepes.

🕊 Crepe Filling #2

1 pound firm white fish, in chunks
1 cup dry white wine
1 tablespoon onion, finely minced
1 tablespoon dried parsley
1 teaspoon salt
1 small can shrimp
1 small can mushrooms, drained
1 small can crab meat
1 cup evaporated milk
3 tablespoons cornstarch

Bring the wine, onion, parsley, and salt to a boil and poach the fish in pieces no larger than walnuts. Rinse and drain the shrimp and flake the crab. Measure the liquid after poaching and add water, including the liquid from the mushrooms, to make two cups. Add a small amount of the liquid to the cornstarch to make a paste, then thin the paste and add it to a pot in which you have assembled all the other ingredients except the milk. Heat, stirring over medium heat, until the sauce is smooth and thick. Remove it from the heat and stir in the milk. If you like, add a nugget of butter and some grated cheese. Fills 24 crepes.

Breakfast crepes may also be filled with:

- canned corned beef hash, fried crisp
- fried sausages heated with applesauce
- scrambled eggs with cheese sauce or chili sauce
- fresh or well-drained canned fruit
- chicken à la King from a can
- long strips of cheese, folded into hot crepe to melt
- two hard-boiled egg halves per crepe, sauced with salsa
- ripe bananas, sliced lengthwise and fried in butter
- scrambled eggs and refried beans

⚓ Blintzes

1 recipe crepes, saving ¼ cup batter uncooked
about ⅔ cup cottage cheese (see Glossary)
2 eggs
1 teaspoon salt
1 tablespoon sugar (optional)
butter for frying

Thoroughly whisk the eggs, cottage cheese, salt, and sugar. Put a tablespoon of this filling on each crepe, taking care not to overfill. Fold over one side of the circle, then the two opposite sides, sealing as you go with the raw crepe batter. Fold over the remaining flap and seal. Handle the blintz gently as you fry it in butter until browned on both sides. During cooking, the egg in the filling will firm, making the blintzes easier to handle. Real butter is best for flavor and for browning. Serve with strawberry jam and sour cream if you have some.

34

One-Hand Breakfasts

The following recipes are for satisfying and nutritious, but offbeat, breakfast choices which can be eaten at the tiller with one hand. When you're preparing for an overnight passage or several days of bad weather underway, bake these ahead and wrap them individually. They don't have to be cooked, buttered, basted, or beaten. Simply eat and enjoy the energy they provide. Complete the meal with a cup of hot coffee or cocoa if you can manage it.

 ## Bacon Bars

⅔ cup shortening
½ cup honey or sugar
2 eggs
1 teaspoon vanilla
¾ cup flour
1½ cups uncooked oatmeal
½ teaspoon baking soda
1 cup grated cheese such as cheddar
½ cup wheat germ, ground nuts, or ground seeds
cooked crumbled, real bacon (can or jar)

Cream the fat with eggs, honey or sugar, and vanilla. Shake the dry ingredients together in a bag and add to the creamed mixture. The dough will be very thick. Spread it in a cold, well-greased, heavy aluminum skillet with a tight-fitting lid and place over a medium flame with a flame shield. Bake about 20 to 30 minutes or until the edges are brown and begin to shrink away from the sides of the pan and the center is springy to the touch. When it's cool, cut into wedges and wrap individually.

Variations: instead of the bacon and wheat germ, substitute raisins, cut-up dried apricots, soaked and cut-up dried apples, diced fresh apples, or cut-up pitted prunes. If the cheese is omitted, substitute a quarter-cup of soy flour in the flour measure or one-third cup nonfat dry milk, to add protein.

 ## Banana Bars

¾ cup shortening
½ cup brown sugar
1 egg
½ teaspoon salt
½ teaspoon cinnamon
1½ cups mashed bananas
4 cups uncooked oatmeal
½ cup raisins or other moist dried fruit, cut up
½ cup chopped nuts
½ cup unsalted sunflower seeds

Cream the shortening with sugar and egg, then add salt, spices, and bananas. Stir in the dry ingredients and mix well. Spread it in a cold, well-greased, heavy aluminum skillet for which you have a tight-fitting lid. Place it over a medium flame with a flame shield until the edges are browned and the center is firm to the touch. This takes 20 to 30 minutes. For oven baking, use a 9-by-13-inch pan and bake at 375° for about 25 minutes or until the center is springy and the edges are pulling away from the pan sides.

🫘 Molasses Bars

This recipe was given to me in Cozumel by world-sailor Chris Grey. It is a very nourishing, all-in-one breakfast or snack bar.

⅓ cup margarine or butter
½ cup chunky peanut butter
½ cup molasses
½ cup honey
2 teaspoons vanilla
4 eggs
4 cups fortified, high-protein, ready-to-eat cereal
2 cups whole-wheat flour
1 teaspoon baking powder
½ teaspoon salt
¼ teaspoon baking soda
1 cup mashed bananas
1¼ cups chocolate bits
1 cup chopped, salted peanuts

Cream the butters, syrups, and vanilla, adding the eggs one at a time. Mix the dry ingredients together and stir in alternately with the bananas. Fold in the chocolate bits and peanuts. (Substitute sesame seeds, coconut, sunflower seeds.) Bake in 9-by-13-inch pan at 350° about 30 minutes or until firm. For stovetop baking, divide into two batches and bake by indirect Dutch oven method for about 30 minutes. Cool, then cut and wrap individually.

Galley Tips: Breakfast
Saltwater can be used to hard-boil eggs, but it is not recommended for poaching.

Instead of toast, try instant or regular grits with a dab of butter and a sprinkling of sugar with sunny-side-up eggs.

Powdered diet egg substitute (Eggstra), granular egg-nog mix in a jar, and canned eggnog all make passable French toast. Do not soak the bread completely.

Canned luncheon meat, fried in butter until brown and crisp, is a good substitute for bacon or sausage.

Tender Chunk ham, cut into wedges and tossed in a skillet with butter until browned, makes a good breakfast meat.

Try poaching eggs in canned pizza sauce.

Add two or three eggs per cup of leftover cold rice and fry in butter like pancakes. Serve with syrup.

Fry canned corned-beef hash in butter until crisped, make nests with the back of a spoon, and break an egg into each hole. Cover and bake until eggs begin to firm.

On cold night-watches, hard-boil a couple of eggs before you start your watch and put one, while still hot, in each side pocket of your foul weather gear. They'll serve as hand-warmers at first and make nutritious snacks in the wee hours.

Make delicious toast from any bread (yeast bread, banana bread, leftover biscuits) by buttering and frying until brown.

5. SANDWICHES

All of us, in galleys large and small, rely on sandwiches for lunches and snacks but on the go, when fresh bread isn't always available, sandwiches aren't always that simple.

Here is my collection of sandwich ideas, with suggestions on how they can be served either hot or cold.

The Mealwich

Any sandwich can be transformed into a hot, one-pot meal by French-toasting it. Dip the entire sandwich into a mixture of eggs, milk, and seasonings. Then fry it in butter until it's browned on both sides. The mealwich is best made with pasty fillings like deviled ham, Carnation's Spreadables, or egg salad, which help hold them together while you dip and fry. To make an unusual homemade filling, grind together ham or Spam with cheese, and moisten with well-drained canned pineapple. Make sandwiches and wrap ahead of time. Then if the weather turns cold, you get weathered in, or you simply want a heartier meal, go through the toasting step.

Serve hot sandwiches with a packaged cheese sauce, or a

cream Soup for One full strength. This turns it into a knife-and-fork meal.

Variations: add a few tablespoons of ketchup to the egg-milk mixture used for dipping, add thyme to dip used for fish (including tuna) sandwiches, sprinkle dill weed into the dip for egg salad sandwiches. Serve French-toasted peanut butter and jelly sandwiches for breakfast, lunch, or dinner. Add crumbled bacon for extra flavor.

The Unwich

Carry taco shells to fill with canned Sloppy Joe, or make big crepes to fill burrito-style and then fold to eat from the hand. Fill packaged ice cream cones with a moist salad made from canned corned beef, well-drained canned vegetables, and a binding of yogurt or salad dressing. When you bake Boston brown bread or other can-baked recipes, place a peeled hard-boiled egg in the center of the dough. When it's turned out of the can you'll have a ready-made egg sandwich. (Make sure the can is no more than two-thirds full or it will overflow during rising.) Cold leftover cabbage rolls also make a good unwich to eat from the hand. Try them with a soy sauce dip.

The Open Face

Here is how I make one-slice sandwiches without a broiler. Spread bread with butter, margarine, or bacon fat, and arrange fat-side-down in a big, heavy skillet. With squeezing, my Club Aluminum skillet will hold four slices of store bread; so will most electric frypans. If you need seconds, assemble them on a sheet of waxed paper to cook later.

Drizzle the bread with mustard or salad dressing and stack with tidbits: whole green beans or asparagus spears, sliced sweet onion, coins of Vienna sausage, rings of hard-cooked egg, sliced tomato, halved artichoke hearts from a can, mushroom caps, slivers of canned ham, etc. Top with a slice of cheese or generous amount of grated soft cheese. Cover skillet and place over low

40

fire until bread bottom is crisply browned and cheese is melted. Watch closely so bread doesn't burn before cheese melts.

☜ The Bunwich

This is best made in port when you can get good bakery hamburger buns or rolls, but it also works with galley-made English muffins. The important filling ingredient is the grated cheese. Grind salami, ham, or bologna, or mash corned beef. Mix with a hearty portion of grated cheddar and moisten with a little relish or pickle juice. Add some minced sweet onion, bind with just enough chili sauce, ketchup, or yogurt to moisten, and fill buns or muffins very generously. If you prefer your sandwiches hot, wrap them tightly in foil, place the packets on a rack in a heavy skillet, lid, and heat over a low flame until the sandwiches are heated through. The cheese melts, giving the hot sandwich a completely different character from the cold version.

Here are some other ideas:

• Spread peanut butter with jelly, honey, crumbled bacon, sliced banana, or applesauce on canned Boston brown bread.

• Mash sardines, moisten with lemon juice, spread on saltines, and sprinkle with grated Parmesan.

• Mash corned beef, moisten with chili sauce, and spread on Swedish rye crackers.

• Cover slices of canned Boston brown bread with baked beans from a can and layer with thin slices of canned Vienna sausage. Crown with a little sweet relish.

• Split leftover cornbread and spread with heated chili con carne from a can.

• Smooth pineapple-cheese spread from a jar onto crisp round crackers and sprinkle with chopped peanuts.

• Split leftover breakfast biscuits and butter them. Make sandwiches with asparagus spears from a can and sauce them with heated cheddar cheese soup, undiluted.

• Carry cans of date and nut bread to spread with pimento cheese spread from a jar.

• Check supermarket shelves for a great variety of canned spreadables: liverwurst, deviled ham, chicken spread or corned beef spread.

• Save time and mess in the busy galley by buying peanut butter and jelly mixed in the same jar.

• Look over the cheese shelves for long-lasting, spreadable sandwich cheeses. There are jars, aerosol cans, and plastic squeeze packets, and all carry without refrigeration.

• Use plastic squeeze bottles for mustard, ketchup, chili sauce, and honey. If you cruise *with* refrigeration, use them for margarine (Squeeze Parkay) and mayonnaise, too. Camping supply sources also sell tubes which can be used for heavier pastes such as peanut butter and jelly. These make sandwich-making quicker and eliminate washing knives and spreaders.

• Alfalfa sprouts are indispensable to the cruising sandwich-maker. Use them in place of lettuce we use so commonly in sandwiches in port. (Buy sprouting seeds at natural foods stores, and ask there for sprouting instructions.)

• Make a French dip for roast beef sandwiches by serving with a cup of prepared onion soup from can or package. Add a splash of sherry if you like.

• Create a passable Reuben by adding a forkful of canned sauerkraut to a sandwich made from canned corned beef and a slice of cheese. Butter outsides and pan fry until bread is toasty brown and cheese is melted.

• Mashed avocado, which you can have in the iceless galley up to ten days from port, can be used alone in a sandwich or with meats or fish as a binding.

• If you're used to celery in egg salad or tuna salad sandwiches, and have none, try diced sweet onion, grated cabbage, diced cabbage core, diced water chestnuts, chopped apple, chopped nuts, or cut-up pickles to add crunch.

• For speedier egg salad sandwiches, scramble eggs firm and then chop.

• When you are making sandwiches ahead of time, to be eaten some hours later, butter both slices of bread thoroughly to keep sandwich filling from soaking into bread.

• Although many cruising sailors carry opened mayonnaise and salad dressing without refrigeration, it's not recommended because these two foods make excellent culturing media for organisms which can cause food poisoning. Use yogurt or fresh-made salad dressings to moisten sandwich fillings, or buy salad dressing in the small, eight-ounce (one-cup) jars which can be used up in one day.

• Turn any meat sandwich into a hot meal by saucing it with hot gravy from a can, jar, or mix.

• No matter how steamy the weather, it's always a safe bet to carry sandwiches made from buttered bread, mustard and slabs of cheese. If you have leftovers at the end of the day and want to make them into a hearty supper dish, arrange the cheese sandwiches (cut if necessary to fit them all in) to cover the bottom of a heavy, cold, well-buttered skillet. Whisk together two cups milk with two or three eggs and pour over the sandwiches. Cover skillet and bake over low flame until custard is set. This custard treatment goes well with other sandwich flavors too.

6. MAIN DISHES

You'll note that I've used a number of recipes which call for beef, pork, turkey, chicken, and other meats which you may have difficulty finding in cans. The simple secret in having a varied cruising diet is to can all types of meat yourself. In most cases you save money, but you also eliminate additives, excess fat, fillers, and chemicals that many commercially canned meats contain. (For information on canning, see Chapter 19.)

Naturally, many of the following recipes can and should be made with fresh ingredients when you have them. But when you have fresh foods, you can also turn to other cookbooks. It is the aim of this chapter to suggest balanced, varied, and tasty main dishes which can be made from stowed supplies.

You'll note that in many cases I haven't indicated how many servings the recipe will provide because so often such indicators are meaningless. A pint of home-canned meat is about a pound of meat, which can serve two if you're in a carnivorous mood and four or even eight if you add plenty of fillers and stretchers. Generally, servings are figured by nutritionists at four ounces boneless meat per person. Rice trebles in bulk when cooked so you'll get six half-cup servings from one cup of raw rice. Pasta doubles in cooking so you'll get four half-cup servings from one cup of raw macaroni. Noodles, which are difficult to measure raw, will provide six to eight servings from an eight-ounce package.

If you are new to cooking, become a label reader. Often the

servings are spelled out for you (e.g., "contains four four-ounce servings"). Each cruise is different and crews vary, too, so count on practice, common sense, and a good supply of filling extras, and you'll always have enough food at your table.

Eight-Crew Stew

1 medium onion, diced
¼ cup butter or 2 tablespoons oil
8 medium potatoes, whole
2 cans (12 ounces each) roast beef loaf
1 medium bottle (12 to 16 ounces) ketchup
salt and pepper to taste

Chop the onion and fry it in butter or oil until it's translucent. Add the potatoes and just enough water to cook them. Simmer until the potatoes are tender (ten minutes in pressure cooker for whole potatoes). Add the meat, which has been cut into eight chunks, ketchup, and seasonings. Does the large amount of ketchup surprise you? That's what adds the delicious tang to this dish. Still, it's quite spicy so don't add other vegetables. Serve them on the side.

Wieners and Kraut

1 one-pound package hot dogs or equivalent in canned hot
    dogs, Vienna sausage, or canned cocktail wieners
2 one-pound cans sauerkraut
2 whole cloves
1 apple, chopped (substitute soaked, dried apple)
a pinch of caraway seeds
1 medium onion, chopped
1 can beer
potatoes (optional)

Drain the kraut well and put it in a heavy saucepan or pressure cooker with the onion, apple, and spices. Cover with beer and simmer one hour or pressure cook ten minutes. Add the franks and heat thoroughly. This is.very good with instant or fresh mashed potatoes. If you prefer to make it a one-pot meal, add one scrubbed potato per person before cooking the kraut or add one or two one-pound cans of well-drained canned potatoes with the hot dogs.

⚓ Burgoo for the Crew

This huge, lobster-pot-size meal feeds a crew of 15. It is ideal for dockside parties or beach potluck suppers.

1 quart canned boneless chicken or meat from two whole canned chickens
1 pint canned beef cubes
1 pint canned veal or pork cubes
2 one-pound cans whole potatoes
1 one-pound can sliced carrots
1 one-pound can whole onions
1 one-pound can okra
1 one-pound can celery
1 one-pound can lima beans
1 one-pound can tomatoes
3 quarts water including juices from meats and vegetables
1 can (about 1¼ cups) tomato purée
1 teaspoon pepper
2 tablespoons salt
1 teaspoon chili powder
2 tablespoons dried parsley flakes
1½ teaspoons dry mustard
a dash of Tabasco sauce

Simmer it all together for about an hour, allowing flavors to blend. It's even better made early in the day and rewarmed. Ladle into soup bowls and serve with a crusty bread.

Sweet and Sour Bean Treat

1 can (12 ounces) luncheon meat
1 one-pound can kidney beans
⅓ cup brown sugar
¼ cup vinegar
1 teaspoon prepared mustard
1 tablespoon cornstarch

Slice the canned meat according to the number of servings needed, and arrange it on serving plates. If you can manage it, fry the meat first. If not, the hot beans will heat it. Heat the beans in a medium saucepan. Make a paste with the sugar, mustard, cornstarch, and vinegar and add it to the beans, heating and stirring until the beans are thick and saucy. Some beans are juicier than others, so add water if necessary to keep them from burning. Spoon the beans over the meat. Not only is this a flavor change-of-pace for canned meat, it's a budget stretcher. With the added protein of the beans, this supplies as many as eight servings if necessary.

Dixie One-Dish

2 pounds canned ham
2 one-pound cans sweet potatoes
¼ cup butter, melted
1 can pie-sliced apples
¼ cup brown sugar
½ cup cookie crumbs, preferably ginger snaps

Scrape the coating from the ham and discard it unless you can use it in another dish the same day. Cut the ham into eight slices and arrange them in a roomy, buttered, cold skillet. Mash the sweet potatoes, using about half the melted butter, and spread them over the ham. Arrange the apple slices over the sweet potatoes and sprinkle them with the cookie crumbs. (If you're using bland cookies rather than ginger snaps, add a quar-

48

ter-teaspoon ginger to the crumbs and mix well before adding them.) Drizzle with the remaining butter. Cover and bake over a medium flame until everything is well heated. If a crustier topping is preferred, don't add the crumbs before heating. Fry them in a little butter and sprinkle them on the dish just before presenting it. This dish provides eight people with a quarter-pound of ham each.

Satori Seven-Dish Curry

Gay Thompson aboard the charter schooner *Satori* out of St. Thomas in the Virgin Islands is a resourceful cook who learned the culinary ropes during a sail from California to the Virgins. Although her curry can be made with fresh beef, she has often made it with one of the large Armour beef roasts that come in cans. I've made her recipe using my own home-canned beef squares. It's an ideal dazzler for company because you can dish up all the condiments in advance, make the curry ahead of time, and cook only the rice at mealtime.

> about 2½ pounds beef
> 2 or 3 cups gravy (canned or homemade)
> 3 tablespoons curry powder or to taste
> 1 large can mushroom stems and pieces
> 3 cups cooked rice

Begin with squares of cooked beef and make the gravy from the juices, from a packet of mix, or by heating canned gravy. Assemble all the ingredients except the rice and heat in a roomy saucepan.

To serve, center the galley table with the condiments. Place rice on each plate, top with the curried beef, and pass the condiments so each crewman can flavor the curry as he pleases.

Condiments include any or all of the following (Gay uses seven):

> crumbled, cooked bacon
> grated or shredded cheese
> alfalfa sprouts or shredded lettuce
> finely chopped sweet onion
> shredded coconut
> roasted or raw almonds
> raisins
> canned pineapple chunks, drained
> chutney

⚓ Lamb Curry

> 2 tablespoons butter
> 1 large onion, diced
> 2 teaspoons curry powder
> 1 tablespoon flour
> 2 pounds (1 quart home-canned) lamb cubes
> ½ cup raisins
> ½ cup slivered almonds
> 1½ cups yogurt
> hot rice

Sauté the onion in butter, add curry, and cook until the onion is soft. Make a paste by adding a little of the lamb juice to the flour. If the lamb is exceedingly juicy, use two tablespoons flour. Combine all ingredients except the yogurt and rice, and simmer until it's thick and smooth. Remove it from the heat and stir in the yogurt. Serve immediately over hot rice.

🐟 Shipped Beef

2½-ounce jar dried chipped beef
1 small onion, minced
1 one-pound can tomatoes
8 ounces cheddar cheese
1 or 2 eggs

Heat the tomatoes, onion, and shredded beef and simmer, covered, five minutes. Grate the cheese or substitute a can of cheese soup or a small jar of Cheez Whiz. Remove the tomato mixture from the heat and add the cheese. Heat again, but take care not to boil, until the cheese is well melted and blended. Remove from heat and quickly stir in the egg(s) until they set. Serve over toast, pancakes, or rice.

Chipped Beef Puff

Juggling bread supplies has always been a problem in my galley because homemade bread has to be eaten quickly before it molds. This dish helps use up the bread. Or, you can cut the bread into cubes and dry it for later use in this recipe.

½ loaf fresh or dry bread
walnut-size chunk of butter
1 small jar dried chipped beef
2 tablespoons prepared mustard
4 eggs
3 cups milk

Butter a heavy pan or pressure cooker very heavily and reserve any remaining butter to dot over the mixture. Pile the cubed bread into the pan and sprinkle with well-shredded dried beef. Combine the eggs, milk, and mustard and blend thoroughly. Pour over the bread and let it stand about an hour until the bread is thoroughly soaked. Cover the pan and bake over a low flame with a flame shield until the custardy mixture is just barely set. Remove from heat, let stand a few minutes, and serve. For oven baking, use a casserole dish and bake about one hour at 350° or until custard is set.

Ham-and-Egg Frittata

It's a hearty supper, or it can be served for breakfast or brunch. Frittata is just another way of saying omelet, and it is often made with vegetables instead of meat. To make it a vegetarian main dish, skip the ham and add a vegetable, such as well-drained, canned yellow squash.

6 eggs
1 medium onion, diced
3 tablespoons oil
salt, pepper
1 one-pound can sliced potatoes
½ to 1 cup finely diced ham

Beat the eggs along with a tablespoon or two of water. Sizzle the onion in the oil, then add canned potatoes that you have drained, rinsed, and drained again. Stir in the ham. After everything has been well heated, spread it evenly in the pan, turn the heat to low, and add the beaten eggs. Cover and let steam about ten minutes or until the eggs are set. Serve in wedges. This makes four big servings.

🐚 Snitz and Knepp

1½-pound canned ham
1 can pie-sliced apples or 1½ to 2 cups cooked dried apples
2 tablespoons brown sugar
1 cup biscuit mix
water

Slice the ham or cut it into large squares. Add water to the apples until they are the consistency of soupy stew. Stir the ham and sugar into the apples in a roomy saucepan and bring to a slow boil. Add enough water to the biscuit mix to form a thick dough and drop it by teaspoons into the bubbling apple mixture. Cook ten minutes uncovered. Add more water if necessary to keep the bottom from burning, keeping the mixture boiling. Then cover the pan and cook ten minutes more. Spoon the apple-ham mixture over the dumplings to serve.

🦐 Chop-Chop Suey

1 pint (1 pound) home-canned chicken, beef, pork, or veal
2 tablespoons cornstarch
water
2 teaspoons MSG
2 teaspoons granular chicken or beef bouillon
½ teaspoon gravy browner such as Gravy Master
a splash of sherry (optional)
1 large onion, sliced
about 3 tablespoons mung beans, sprouted four days
1 one-pound can mixed Chinese vegetables with water chestnuts

This is my number-one favorite dish made with canned meat because the meat is refreshed so vividly by fresh sprouts and onion. Further contrast is added by the canned water chestnuts and canned Chinese vegetables. It's a dish you can serve aboard the humblest boat, not just to fellow sailors but to shore folk and to the people from the big yacht next door, with pride. We much prefer brown rice with this, although white rice is more traditional. Pass the noodles separately, for use as a crisp topping. No salt is used in either the chop suey or the rice because we sprinkle the chop suey with soy sauce, which is very salty.

Drain the canned meat into a two-cup measure and make a paste with the cornstarch. Add the MSG, bouillon, gravy browner, and sherry. Add water, including the liquid from the canned vegetables, to make two cups. Heat a few tablespoons of oil in a roomy skillet or wok and stir-fry the onion until it begins to look translucent. Add the sprouts and stir-fry until they wilt. Then add the meat and continue stir-frying over a high flame. Reduce the heat and add the drained vegetables, heat, add the cornstarch mixture, and continue stirring and cooking just until it's thick and clear. Overcooking makes the vegetables mushy. Ideally, the onions and sprouts should have plenty of crunch. Serve over Chinese noodles or unsalted rice, and pass the soy sauce.

🐟 Pitch-and-Toss

So many versions of this recipe have been printed and shared, and so many variations are possible, I'm just going to throw out lists of choices so you can let your own imagination, taste, and available foods decide the outcome.

Base:

cream of mushroom, celery, asparagus, chicken, or cheese soup *or*
about 1½ cups of your own medium white sauce *or*
instant soup mixed with half the water requirement (do not salt other ingredients) *or*
white sauce from a can or a mix

Meat or fish:

canned tuna, salmon, chicken, turkey, or ham

Extras:

small, well-drained cans of peas, mushrooms, or diced carrots

Starch:

hominy, cooked pasta or rice or canned Chinese noodles

Combine one ingredient from each category in a cold, buttered saucepan. Bake over low heat with shield until heated through. Extra liquid may be needed, especially if you begin with a condensed soup and other low-moisture ingredients.

Vegetarian Main Dishes

Tipsy Black Beans

2 cups dried black (turtle) beans
6 cups water
1 large onion, chopped
2 cloves garlic, mashed
3 tablespoons oil
1 bay leaf
1 teaspoon thyme
1 teaspoon oregano
salt, pepper to taste
½ cup rum
yogurt
cooked rice

Early in the day, preferably over the breakfast fire, start the beans. (Black beans are sold commonly in cities with a Cuban or Caribbean population; in other areas, check specialty stores.) Wash them and, after picking out any bad ones, place them in a pressure cooker with the water. Bring up to pressure, remove from heat, and let stand. If you light the stove again for lunch or a coffee break, bring the beans up to pressure again and set aside. It takes some practice, but most dried beans can be cooked this way, using very little fuel. Before dinner, sauté the onion in oil and add the onion and spices to the beans. Add half the rum and bring the pan up to full pressure for ten minutes. (Total cooking time will depend on the pre-cooking you've done during the day.) Just before serving, adjust the seasonings and stir in the remaining rum. Serve over white rice, and top each serving with a dollop of yogurt.

⚓ Chickpea One-Pot

1 large onion, diced
1 one-pound can zucchini in tomato sauce
1 one-pound can chickpeas (garbanzo beans)
1 one-pound can hominy
grated cheese

Sauté the onion in a little butter or oil until it's soft, then add the vegetables. Season to taste. Serve in shallow bowls, mounded with grated cheese, with cornbread on the side.

Chickpea Meatballs

Deep-frying is an excellent way to vary cruising menus and to bring crisp texture to a canned-foods meal. Traditionally, these meatballs are served in pita bread sandwiches, but they're equally good as a meat substitute with other vegetables added to the plate.

1 can (2 cups) chickpeas, drained and mashed
⅔ cup fresh whole-wheat bread crumbs
1 medium onion, diced fine
1 or 2 eggs
2 or 3 cloves garlic, mashed
½ teaspoon baking soda
1 tablespoon lemon juice
½ teaspoon salt
1 tablespoon dried parsley
1 teaspoon curry powder
oil for deep-frying

Mash all ingredients together to make a smooth paste. Using two teaspoons which you've dipped in cold water, drop balls of the mixture into hot oil. (350° oil will brown a cube of fresh bread in about 30 seconds.) Fry until crisp and browned, and drain on absorbent paper. Serve with:

Tahini Sauce

1 cup sesame oil
juice of 3 lemons
1 tablespoon dried parsley
1 clove of garlic, mashed
a dash of salt

Shake all the ingredients together in a tightly lidded jar and serve as a dip with the meatballs. Remove the garlic after 12 hours. The sauce will keep three days or more without refrigeration.

Quiche

Although quiche can be made with bits of canned ham or chicken or with crumbled bacon, it also makes an ideal vegetarian dish because even meat eaters love it.

Crust:

1 cup white or whole-wheat flour
½ cup butter or margarine
grated cheese, chopped almonds, or ground pecans (optional)

Melt the butter and mix in the flour with a fork, adding more flour if the mixture looks too oily (both fats and flours vary). With your fingers, press this evenly to the bottom and sides of a pie pan that fits into your stovetop oven. Preheat the oven while you mix the filling.

Filling:

1 medium onion, diced
2 or 3 eggs
salt and pepper to taste
1 to 1½ cups yogurt or milk

about 1 cup grated cheddar cheese
a sprinkle of nutmeg
about 1 cup cooked vegetables
1 small can mushrooms, drained
imitation bacon bits (optional)

The sizes and depths of pie pans vary so much, as do the amounts of vegetables different cooks like to use in quiche, that I've been deliberately vague about the amounts of egg and yogurt to use. I begin by whisking together two eggs and one cup milk or yogurt. (If your homemade yogurt is especially tangy, you may prefer to use part milk.) Strew the unbaked pie shell with mushrooms, almost any well-drained cooked vegetables, bits of meat, if you want, and some imitation bacon bits, if you like them. Sprinkle with the onion, seasonings, and grated cheese. Then spread with the egg mixture. If the pan is not filled enough, whisk together another egg and a half-cup or so of milk, and add it. Bake in your stovetop oven (I use the indirect Dutch oven method) until the filling is set and the crust is browned around the edges. Let stand for at least five minutes, then cut into wedges and serve.

🐚 Beer Fondue

If you cook this in a very heavy, heat-retaining pot, it won't be necessary to keep it over a fondue cooker at the table. To make individual servings in heavy weather when you can't gather around the pot to dip the bread, fill bowls with bread cubes and spoon the fondue over them. While more authentic cheese fondues use other cheese and white wine, this is both delicious and easy for the galley cook, and cheddar cheese is a good keeper.

1 pound medium cheddar cheese
2 tablespoons cornstarch
a dash of dry mustard
1 clove garlic
a can of beer
1 loaf of bread

Grate the cheese, which can be a mixture of cheeses if you have bits to use up, and toss it with the cornstarch. Rub a very heavy saucepan with the mashed garlic, and discard the pulp. Heat the beer until it begins to steam, but keep it from boiling as you add the cheese, cup by cup, until the mixture is smooth. Place the pan on hot-pads in the center of the table, swathe it with a clean towel to help retain the heat, and dip into it with cubes of a crusty bread speared on forks. If the mixture becomes too thick, reheat gently until it thins to the right consistency again.

The Cream of the Cruise

Versatile, filling, economical, and easy are the words that sum up serving creamed something on almost anything. By using one basic cream-sauce mix, which can be made in quantity ahead of time, you can come up with endless combinations. Creamed foods make colorful, dollar-stretching entrées, and they provide texture contrast by balancing the soupy sauce with a crunchy item such as Chinese noodles from a can. On a long cruise, when you are eating out of cans and packages, this change-of-pace becomes very important. The sauce can also be used to give a new look to tiresome canned vegetables served as a side dish with meat or fish.

Basic Cream-Sauce Mix:

2 heaping tablespoons cornstarch
1 teaspoon chicken bouillon granules or salt
⅔ cup nonfat dry milk
½ teaspoon MSG (optional)

Multiply as many times as you wish, mixing ingredients very well and storing in an airtight container. For each cup of medium white sauce, combine a generous one-third cup of the mix with a cup of water. Stir over medium heat until mixture thickens. Add a walnut-size chunk of butter, if you want, plus herbs suitable to the dish. When using the creamed food as a main dish, plan a half-cup white sauce per person.

To the basic hot cream sauce you may add:

- chopped hard-boiled eggs, one per person
- cooked, drained mixed vegetables, any combination
- canned mushroom stems and pieces, well drained
- canned salmon, tuna, ham, chicken, or turkey
- dried chipped beef, rinsed in a little boiling water to remove excess salt
- dried cod or other salt fish, soaked if necessary to remove excess salt
- flaked, cooked fish, shrimp, lobster, crab, or cut-up scallops
- canned corned beef

A small can of peas and carrots, well drained and added to any of the above, will extend the dish and add color.

Serve the hot, creamed mixture over:

- toast
- white rice
- corn chips
- Chinese noodles

- brown rice
- potato sticks
- instant mashed potatoes
- grits
- bean sprouts
- fresh, grated cabbage
- any cooked noodle product
- French-cut green beans
- any cooked pasta
- canned julienne carrots, rinsed and drained
- leftover pancakes, biscuits, French toast or waffles
- cornbread which has been split, buttered and toasted in skillet
- unsugared ready-to-eat cereal
- leftover bread stuffing, formed in patties and fried in butter
- leftover corn fritters, split
- cooked barley or other grain
- packaged patty shells
- canned, whole potatoes which have been rinsed, drained, and quartered

Note: When using salted snacks as a base, beware of excess saltiness, particularly in combination with canned corned beef or salt fish. Make a special white-sauce mix, omitting salt.

After arranging servings on plates, garnish with:

- crumbled, hard-boiled egg yolk
- crumbled, cooked bacon
- freeze-dried chives or dried parsley
- salad seasoning such as McCormick Salad Supreme
- splash of soy sauce or sherry
- dollop of ketchup or sour cream

- half a canned artichoke heart
- strips of pimento from a jar
- chopped, fresh onion
- sliced, stuffed olives
- chopped black olives, well drained
- grated cheese
- canned French-fried onion rings
- pat of butter
- sprinkling of dill weed, caraway seed, or toasted sesame seed
- croutons
- bread crumbs fried in butter
- fresh onion rings, fried in butter until soft
- crushed potato chips or other snacks
- marble-size balls of deviled ham
- chopped nuts

Galley Tips: Main Dishes

Semi-condensed Soup-for-One, heated in the can and used full strength, makes a smooth and tasty sauce for meats.

To liven and extend a commercially canned main dish such as chicken and dumplings, beef stew, or chili, heat in a skillet. Then combine a half-cup of grated dry cheese, one egg, and one cup milk and pour over the hot dish. Cover and cook over low heat a few minutes more until topping sets.

Make a glaze for canned luncheon meats or ham by combining a half-cup ketchup, two tablespoons brown sugar or molasses, and one teaspoon prepared mustard. Both ketchup and mustard, by the way, keep many days without refrigeration.

It's best to home-can meats without salt. It isn't needed as part of the preservation process. Then, when you add salty commercial soups and sauces, the total result is not oversalted.

Make homemade or commercially canned main dishes more filling and hearty by adding a cornbread topping. Heat the food in a skillet, then spoon over it one package of cornbread mix, prepared according to package directions. Cover and keep simmering until cornbread is springy and set.

There's no need to cook rice, macaroni, noodles, or spaghetti separately. Simply add one cup extra water to the meat sauce recipe for each four ounces of noodles, rice, or pasta to be cooked. Bring to a boil, add starch, and cook until tender.

When you buy canned ham, make sure it is the type that is not meant to be refrigerated! Read the label.

Make a sauce for canned ham with preserves, marmalade, or a fruity pie filling from a can.

Use commercially canned corned beef in many roles: Sloppy Joes, spaghetti sauce, corned beef and cabbage, hash and eggs, and even meatloaf (use two eggs as a binder). Salt carefully—the saltiness of the beef varies.

Make crusty "hamburgers" from almost any home-canned or commercially canned meat or fish which can be mashed. Add a fresh egg, chopped onion, and leftover mashed potatoes. Form into patties, dredge in bread crumbs, and fry in hot oil until browned and set. Great for tuna, corned beef, chicken.

Tinned cream is sold in many parts of the world (see "Milk" in the glossary). It makes a rich and flavorful gravy with almost any meat or fish. Try it when you're cruising Europe, Down Under, or the Indies.

Refresh canned main-dish meals, such as beef stew, by sautéing a chopped onion in a little butter before heating the stew.

Add a winy tang to beef stew by adding syrup from canned fruit, or a little grape juice.

Turn sliced Spam or other luncheon loaf into a crispy cutlet by dipping slices in egg, then bread crumbs. Fry in hot oil until browned.

To reshape your own or commercially canned meats and fish into patties or a meatloaf requires something to make it all stick together again, which is why so many meat recipes here call for fresh eggs.

Extend any canned or fresh meat by adding mashed, cooked beans. A large can of tuna (13 ounces) plus a well-drained, one-pound can of kidney beans, mashed to a paste, mixed with seasonings and egg, and dipped into crumbs before frying in oil will make six to ten princely, protein-packed burgers.

Although there is now a stovetop pizza mix on the market, you can make any homemade or boxed pizza in a heavy, lidded skillet atop the stove. Use a biscuit mix or yeast-dough base, well pressed into a cold, greased skillet. Top with tomato sauce, favorite pizza flavorings, and cheese, cover, and place over medium heat. Use a flame shield to prevent burning in the middle. The pizza is done when it browns around the edges.

7. FROM PASTA TO POTATOES

"Serve over rice or spaghetti." "Serve with boiled potatoes." "Spoon over mashed potatoes." Time and again, cruising
recipes end with these words. To the rushed, energy-burning
crew, starches are a staff of life. They will be the unsung but
ubiquitous accompaniment for almost every meal prepared in
your galley.

To the voyaging sailor, potatoes are one of the few fresh
foods which can be kept on hand week after week. Rice and
pasta will keep indefinitely if kept dry. Instant mashed potatoes
bought in tins can keep for months. Rice can feed more people,
cost less, and use less stowage space than any other food.

Although the classic galley meal is prepared all in one pot,
there are times when you want separate courses of meat or fish,
starch, and a vegetable on your plate. Still, you want to cut down
on cooking time and burner use.

Here's how. Instruction books call for cooking whole potatoes in the pressure cooker for ten minutes, followed by imme-
diate cooling under cold, running water. Instead, cook them five
to seven minutes and set aside. Cooking will continue while
pressure reduces to normal and your burner is freed for frying
fish or burgers. If you have a small insulated cooler, such as the
one-gallon Igloo, potatoes can also be hurried off the burner.
Cook until almost tender, transfer potatoes and cooking water to
a cooler or ice bucket which has been preheated with boiling
water, and lid tightly until mealtime. Most such coolers make

attractive servers, too. Just make sure the one you use has been engineered for hot as well as cold foods.

Rice cooks in a pressure cooker in no time at all. Add two parts of water to one part of white rice, add sufficient salt, and bring it all up to full pressure. Remove from the burner and set aside until mealtime or at least until pressure has equalized. The water will be absorbed and the rice tender. Brown rice cooks in ten minutes on the burner using this method. Both types of rice can be cooked directly in the cooker, using two parts water to one part rice. Or you can improvise a rice steamer. Make an aluminum foil cup with your fist, fill it with rice, and float it in about an inch of water in the pressure cooker. Add half the usual water measurement to the rice in the foil. The rest of the water needed will be absorbed from the steam. Bring up to full pressure and cook one minute for white rice, 15 minutes for brown. Remove from the burner and serve after pressure goes down. Shorten the cooking times somewhat if you like a drier rice or if the waiting time will be very long after the pressure recedes. The other advantage to this method is that there is no pan to wash. The remaining water can be used for washing dishes.

Potatoes can be cooked in water that is up to 50 percent sea water, depending on how much water you use. Just keep in mind that there are about three tablespoons of salt per quart of sea water. Rice and pastas, which absorb much more of their cooking water, should be cooked in a far weaker sea water mix. If you are trying to be very sparing with fresh water, use slightly more sea water by eliminating salt in gravies and sauces which will be served with the starch course.

🦐 Power's Out Macaroni

Make this hearty salad a few hours before mealtime, to allow flavors to blend. Because it contains no mayonnaise, there is no reason to refrigerate it unless you'll be holding it overnight. To make this a main-dish meal, add a can of well-drained tuna just before serving.

8 ounces macaroni, uncooked
1 small jar sweet pickles, chopped
½ cup bottled Italian dressing
1 small can peas, drained
1 small sweet onion, minced
1 cup cubed process cheese

Cook the marcaroni until it's tender. Drain and immediately toss the hot macaroni with the other ingredients except the cheese. Add cheese just before serving.

Easy-Cheesy Macaroni

2 cups any type macaroni (4 cups when cooked)
1 tablespoon butter
1 can cheddar cheese soup
¼ to ½ cup crushed cheese crackers
salt and pepper to taste

Cook the macaroni, drain it, and add the butter, soup, and seasonings. Turn into a serving dish and sprinkle with cracker crumbs. Serve at once.

Macaroni Red-Hot

2 cups macaroni, uncooked
1 cup cubed process cheese
1 one-pound can tomatoes
2 tablespoons Worcestershire sauce
chili powder to taste
salt and pepper to taste

Cook the macaroni until tender, drain, and fold in remaining ingredients. Cover the pan and bake over medium flame, with shield, until the liquid is absorbed and the cheese is melted.

Macaroni and Toothpicks

This texture contrast will be especially welcome if you are eating a lot of canned food. Potato sticks are salted, so don't add any salt or sea water to the macaroni.

1 cup macaroni, uncooked
1 tablespoon cornstarch
1 cup milk
1 small can potato sticks
1 tablespoon butter

Cook the macaroni and drain it. Stir the cornstarch into the milk to make a smooth paste, then blend it with the macaroni over a medium flame until the sauce is smooth and thick. Add the butter and seasoning to taste. Just before serving, stir in the potato sticks.

Noodles

Toss six to eight ounces noodles, cooked and drained, with any one of the following garnishes:

- 1 tablespoon butter, ½ cup slivered almonds, and 2 teaspoons poppy seed
- 1 cup fine bread crumbs, browned in 4 tablespoons butter
- 1 packet instant sour cream mix, prepared, plus a splash of Tabasco, a dash of Worcestershire sauce, and salt and pepper to taste
- 4 tablespoons butter and 2 tablespoons dried parsley
- 4 tablespoons butter and 3 tablespoons grated Parmesan or Romano cheese

70

Scrambled Noodles

4 ounces noodles
4 eggs
salt and pepper to taste

Boil the noodles until they are tender, drain quickly, and stir in the beaten eggs all at once. Cover the pan tightly and set it aside for a minute or two. The eggs should set from the heat retained in the pan. If not, return to very low heat until eggs cook. Season to taste. As a main dish, this serves two or three, and it serves five or six as a side dish.

To Ritz Plain Boiled Rice:

- Substitute canned tomatoes for water and add one tablespoon instant onion.
- Sauté almonds in butter until brown, add rice and sauté, then add water and cook.
- Add one tablespoon dried parsley flakes before cooking; grated cheese just before serving.
- Use one or two beef or chicken bouillon cubes with the water.
- Substitute orange juice for water, add grated orange rind and a sprinkling of dried celery flakes.
- Drain canned pineapple chunks and stretch juice with water to required measurement. Cook all together with rice.
- For each two cups of raw rice, add one package dehydrated chicken-rice or beef-rice soup mix. Add no more salt or sea water.
- Substitute tomato juice for water measurement. Add instant onion and dried green bell pepper.
- Cook one soup-can rice with one soup-can water and one can concentrated soup.

71

- For a quick rice dessert, combine three-quarters-cup raw rice with one and a half cups water, a half-cup raisins, and a half-cup sugar in pressure cooker. Cook, then add a dash of nutmeg and half a teaspoon vanilla.

- Mince an onion and sauté in two tablespoons butter or oil in pressure cooker. Add one teaspoon or more curry powder and one cup raw rice. Sauté, then add two cups water and cook.

- Starting with three cups hot, cooked rice, stir in two cups prepared mincemeat, two tablespoons butter, and two tablespoons brandy. Serve with grilled pork or lamb. This is good, too, with poultry.

 ## Hot German Potato Salad (Lightning Class)

2 cans sliced potatoes
1 small onion, chopped
1 tablespoon freeze-dried chives
2 tablespoons mock bacon bits or crumbled bacon
2 tablespoons vinegar
4 tablespoons salad oil

Rinse and drain the potatoes, then toss them with the other ingredients over a low flame. Heat through, then serve.

Hot German Potato Salad

6 medium potatoes, cooked and sliced
6 slices bacon
2 tablespoons cornstarch
1 tablespoon sugar
½ cup vinegar
¾ cup water
salt and pepper to taste

Don't add salt to the potatoes or to the sauce until the recipe is assembled because the saltiness of bacons varies. Cut the bacon into small pieces and fry it with the chopped onion until the bacon is crisp and the onion soft. Don't drain off the bacon fat unless you're very calorie-conscious because it does add body and flavor to this dish. Blend the water with the cornstarch and mix it into the bacon mixture. Cook, stirring, over medium heat until the sauce thickens. Boil it for one minute, then toss the cooked potatoes with the sauce until they are evenly coated. Serve hot. Note: most conventional recipes call for cooking potatoes whole, then peeling and slicing them. I never peel potatoes because the skins add flavor and color, and I slice them before cooking to save cooking time and fuel.

Cheesy Potatoes

2 cans whole potatoes, in quarters
1 teaspoon prepared mustard
1 can cheddar cheese soup
a dash of paprika for garnish

Drain, rinse, and drain again the canned potatoes. (Rinsing helps remove the tinny taste.) Then mix all ingredients together in a heavy saucepan and cook, covered, over a low flame until everything is heated through. Do not boil.

Dilled Potatoes

Scrub new potatoes well (or, with older potatoes, peel away a strip around the middle) and boil until tender. Toss with lots of butter and a sprinkling of dill weed. The perfect accompaniment for fish.

Lemon Potatoes

Scrub and quarter potatoes, and cook until fork tender. Salt and pepper to taste. Cut half a lemon in quarters, squeeze over potatoes, then add lemon pieces. Toss with lots of butter until potatoes are well coated. Serve hot with fish and additional lemon slices.

Caraway Potatoes

Scrub and quarter potatoes and boil, with one quartered onion for every two potatoes, until potatoes are tender. Add a generous hunk of butter, and pepper heavily with caraway seeds. Toss to coat potatoes evenly.

Colcannon

This easy Irish classic combines potatoes and vegetables in one dish. Traditionally made with fresh mashed potatoes, it is easily made with instant potatoes, which are revived by the fresh cabbage and onions. To make this a single-dish meal, add a can of tuna, well drained.

> **1 medium onion, halved and sliced**
> **2 or 3 large cabbage leaves, coarsely sliced**
> **instant mashed potatoes according to package directions**
> **   for the number of people you are serving**
> **milk, butter, and salt**
> **1 can tuna (optional)**
> **a dash of nutmeg and pepper**

Boil the onion and cabbage leaves in the amount of water required to cook the instant potatoes you serve. When the vegetables are tender, stir in the potatoes. Add milk, butter, and salt according to the package directions, and the pepper and nutmeg. Cover and let stand for a few minutes to let the flavors blend.

Gnocchi

Serve these rich and satiny homemade dumplings as a base for almost any stew or creamed food, or serve them Italian-style with canned or bottled spaghetti sauce. The high egg content makes them especially rich and nutritious in a meatless meal.

1 cup butter
1 cup water
1 teaspoon salt (omit this if you use sea water in cooking)
1 cup flour
4 eggs
¼ cup grated Parmesan cheese

Bring the butter, water, and salt to a boil, remove the pan from the heat, and immediately dump in the full cup of flour. Stir until the dough forms a ball, then stir in the eggs one at a time until you have a thick batter. Fold in the cheese. Bring a large kettle of water to the boil, using up to one-third sea water if you wish. Using two teaspoons, flick walnut-size balls of dough into the rapidly boiling water, cooking about a quarter of the total batter in the water each time (do not crowd). After four or five minutes, the dumplings will float to the surface and will feel firm to the touch. Remove them with a slotted spoon and repeat until all the dough is cooked. Serve at once.

Spaetzle

When provisioning for a very long time, I buy few packaged noodles because they take up so much stowage space. These German egg dumplings have the rich, eggy taste of the best homemade noodles. Serve them smothered in beef stroganoff, as a main dish, or tossed with buttered bread crumbs as a side dish.

2 eggs
1½ cups flour
½ cup water
a pinch of salt
¼ teaspoon baking powder

Beat the eggs, then beat in the remaining ingredients to make a thick dough. Heat a pot of water to boiling. Press the batter through a coarse sieve, or through the coarse holes of a cabbage grater, into the rapidly boiling water. Simmer until they are light and floating, and remove them with a draining spoon.

Galley Tips: Pasta & Potatoes

When serving instant mashed potatoes, prepare them first and set aside in a tightly lidded pot wrapped in a heavy towel. This waiting time makes a world of difference.

Potatoes can be baked atop the stove in a lidded, heavy Dutch oven over high heat. Place potatoes on a rack. To shorten baking time, place a clean nail or skewer into each potato.

Give a crusty new interest to bland instant mashed potatoes. Mix in an egg, minced onion, and salt and pepper to taste, and fry in butter until brown.

Instant potato flakes can be used to thicken gravies and stews.

Leftover rice can be mixed with beaten egg and fried in butter to make pancakes. Serve with meat or, at breakfast, with syrup.

Make crunchy French fries by cooking drained, well-dried canned potatoes in deep, hot fat.

To make plain rice or mashed potatoes look more festive on your galley table, place individual portions on plates with an ice cream scoop or other mold such as a one-third-cup measure.

You won't have a pan to wash if you make instant mashed potatoes in a Teflon roasting bag. Stand up the bag in a bowl to keep it upright, then assemble the ingredients according to package directions. Wearing oven mitts, gently knead the bag to mix. The potatoes can be made ahead of time, then reheated by placing the bag in boiling water. Caution: do not seal the top of the bag; steam must escape. To serve, wear oven mitts as you strip the hot potatoes out of the bag into a serving bowl.

8. VEGETABLES

This chapter contains only recipes for vegetables which will be served as a meal accompaniment. For more vegetable recipes, see Chapter 6 for vegetarian entrees and Chapter 7 for potato recipes.

 ## Vegetable Toss-Ups

When you're far from stores and shores, relying heavily on canned goods, there are ways to make canned vegetables more interesting. One is to combine two vegetables, a vegetable and a fruit, or a vegetable with a relish. To serve two people, combine two small cans. To serve four, add a small can to a 16-ounce (#303) can. To serve larger crews, combine two or more 16-ounce cans.

- Add canned mushrooms or small whole onions to green beans or peas.
- Combine canned sweet potatoes with a can of pie-sliced apples or a can of pineapple pie filling.
- Mix canned shredded beets with a jar of sweet and sour red cabbage.
- Heat canned tomatoes with crumbled crackers and serve with grated cheese.
- Rinse, drain, and quarter canned whole potatoes and heat

with cream-style corn. Garnish with real or imitation crumbled bacon.

- For succotash, combine cans of whole kernel corn and canned lima beans.
- If you can find small cans of celery, drain and add to any other canned vegetable.
- If you have fresh acorn squash, tomatoes, or green peppers aboard, use them as vessels to hold canned vegetables. Fill scooped-out tomatoes or peppers with Mexican-style corn, arrange in a lidded skillet with a little water, and steam until fresh vegetables are barely tender. Squash can be baked, cut side down, in a covered skillet over low heat. Fill cavity with applesauce.
- To two cans of heated, drained limas, add one can of pepper pot soup, undiluted.
- Heat a small jar of whole, stuffed olives with whole-kernel corn.
- Serve canned, stewed tomatoes hot, studded with whole ripe olives.
- Add sliced, canned peaches, well drained, to pork and beans.
- Combine small cans of peas, corn, and carrots.
- Rinse and drain canned kidney beans and mix with canned green limas.

Brandied Sweet Potatoes

1 large can (about 3½ cups) sweet potatoes or 6 medium sweet potatoes, peeled and boiled until tender
⅓ cup butter
1 cup brown sugar
½ cup orange juice (or orange drink)
⅓ cup apricot brandy (or ⅓ cup apricot preserves plus ½ teaspoon brandy flavoring)

Drain the canned potatoes, or cook the fresh ones. Combine the other ingredients in a roomy saucepan and stir them over medium heat until they blend to a smooth syrup. Add the potatoes and toss to coat them, heating gently until they are heated through. To serve, garnish with slivered almonds.

Scalloped Celery

Not every supermarket carries it, but there are some brands of canned celery. When you find it, stock up for cruising use.

2 one-pound cans celery
1 can cream of celery soup
2½ cups bread crumbs
2 tablespoons butter
grated hard cheese

Drain the celery well and combine it in a saucepan with the soup. Warm it through, but be careful not to burn it on the bottom because the mixture will be thick. In a small skillet, melt the butter and add the bread crumbs. Fry until the crumbs are a toasty brown. Just before serving, sprinkle the crumbs and then the grated cheese over the dish. This makes six to eight servings.

Lima Beans in Sour Cream

1 package sour-cream sauce mix
1 can cooked green limas
1 small onion, minced
1 tablespoon butter

Prepare the sour cream according to package directions and set it aside. Sauté the onion in butter until translucent, then add the well-drained beans. Heat through, remove from heat, and fold in sour cream. Makes three or four servings.

Beets à l'Orange

1 one-pound can sliced or quartered beets
1 can (about 8 ounces) mandarin oranges
½ cup beet juice
1 tablespoon cornstarch
salt and pepper
a dash of nutmeg
1 tablespoon butter

Drain the beets and save a half-cup of the juice. Drain the oranges and save the juice for fruit drinks. In a medium sauce-pan, stir a little beet juice into the cornstarch to make a smooth paste, then continue adding juice, stirring. Cook over low heat until the mixture is smooth and thickened. Add the butter, stir to melt it, then fold in the orange sections and beets. Heat gently until everything is well warmed. Season to taste.

Variation: use carrots instead of beets.

Sunstruck Cabbage

1 medium head of cabbage
1 teaspoon lemon juice
1 egg, beaten
2 tablespoons butter
salt and pepper to taste

Coarsely slice the cabbage and cook until it's just tender. Drain well. Immediately stir in the other ingredients, replace the lid, and let the pan stand until the egg sets from the heat of the cabbage. Stir, adjust seasonings, and serve at once.

Green Bean Casserole

2 cans green beans, any style
I can cream of mushroom soup
1 can French-fried onion rings

80

This is a very popular recipe for home use, but you assemble it differently on a boat. Cook the green beans in their liquid until they are well heated, drain, and add the soup. Heat gently, turn into a serving dish, and then sprinkle with the onions. For conventional oven baking, the dish can be assembled and baked with the onions on top.

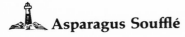 Asparagus Soufflé

2 one-pound cans asparagus
12 saltines
1 can cheddar cheese soup

Drain the asparagus and crush the saltines. Mix everything together in a buttered, heavy saucepan. Lid tightly and heat well over lowest flame.

Greek Vegetable Casserole

¼ cup olive oil
1 medium onion, diced
1 clove garlic, minced
2 potatoes, sliced
1 small can carrots
1 can zucchini in tomato sauce
1 teaspoon oregano
1 teaspoon basil
½ teaspoon cumin
salt and pepper to taste

Sauté the onion and garlic in the oil. Add the potatoes, well-drained carrots, and remaining ingredients. Simmer, covered, until the potatoes are tender, using a flame shield if necessary to keep it from scorching.

🥕 Spinach Pie

Canned spinach is pretty awful, but on very long cruises I always take one or two cans of it because variety becomes so important. Here is one way to make canned spinach more palatable.

1 medium onion, diced
2 tablespoons butter or margarine
2 tablespoons flour or cornstarch
1 cup milk
2 eggs
a dash of pepper
1 one-pound can spinach, very well drained
1 recipe Anti-Roll Pie Crust (see page 151), optional

Sauté the onion in butter until it's translucent. Make a paste with the flour or cornstarch and milk, thin it with the remaining milk, and add it to the onion. Cook, stirring, over medium heat until the sauce is smooth and thickened. Cool 15 minutes, then add the eggs and spinach. Turn this into a buttered pie plate or a pie plate lined with crust, and bake over medium heat in preheated Dutch oven until the filling is set and the crust is brown around the edges.

🥕 Spicy Green Beans

2 tablespoons margarine or butter
2 tablespoons oil
1 teaspoon mustard seeds
1 medium onion, diced
1 teaspoon coriander
2 tablespoons lemon juice
2 one-pound cans green beans
1 eight-ounce can carrots
salt to taste

Heat the butter and oil together in a roomy saucepan and sizzle the mustard seeds until they pop. Stir in the onion and cook it crisp-tender. Add the spices and stir in the well-drained vegetables. Heat through. Makes five cups vegetables.

All-at-Sea Ratatouille

There is no real substitute for fresh vegetables, freshly prepared, but this is the next best thing. (The eggplant appetizer is sold in Italian specialties sections of most large supermarkets. It makes a colorful, tasty addition to other vegetable dishes, too.)

1 medium onion, diced
1 clove garlic, minced
2 tablespoons olive oil
1 one-pound can zucchini in tomato sauce
1 or 2 cans (4 ounces each) eggplant appetizer
1 teaspoon basil
1 tablespoon dried diced green pepper if you have some

Sauté the onion and garlic in hot oil until crisp-tender, then add the remaining ingredients and salt to taste. Heat it through.

Galley Tips: Vegetables
Replace freshlike sweetness in canned vegetables by glazing with one teaspoon sugar after heating. Drain, toss with sugar to coat, and serve.

Vary canned vegetables by serving them creamed. Make a white sauce with one tablespoon cornstarch, one cup milk, and two tablespoons butter. Salt and pepper to taste. Pour over the drained, hot vegetable and cook over low heat, stirring constantly, until the sauce is thickened.

Make any canned vegetable seem more like fresh by adding a fresh onion. Sauté a small diced onion in butter, add the drained vegetable, and heat gently.

Add texture contrast to tired, canned vegetables with a crunchy topping. Use canned French-fried onion rings, bread crumbs fried in butter, or croutons. Add only at the last minute so steam does not turn crunchy to soggy.

Make a fabulous topping for any heated, drained, canned vegetable. Mix equal amounts of mayonnaise or salad dressing and grated cheese—a quarter- to a half-cup of each will do. Spread over heated vegetable in a stove-to-table container and broil the top brown with a propane torch. Work evenly and don't get too close. If you have a broiler, of course, use it.

Create a quick "mystery sauce" for any canned vegetable by mixing a raw egg with a tablespoon or two of grated cheese. Heat the vegetable well, drain thoroughly, and immediately pour in the egg mixture. Leave the pan off the heat but cover it. The egg will soon set. Stir and serve.

9. SAUCES AND GARNISHES

Good cooks know that food reaches the eyes before it hits the taste buds, and that the appearance of food readies the salivary glands for the treat to come. In the limited counter space of our galleys, however, there is no room to prepare and hold extra fillips, no spare burners for simmering sauces, and no refrigerator where we can warehouse the frills we keep on hand at home.

Still, the finishing touch is even more important when you are eating a shortcut meal in cramped quarters. Small, bathroom-size paper cups come in handy for many things in the galley, including serving individual portions of pudding or wine, and little mixing jobs. In my galley, I use them for garnishes, all lined up to be dashed on at the last minute so I won't have to start rummaging in lockers for dashes of paprika or shaved chocolate.

If green will complement the food, I use freeze-dried chives, dried or fresh parsley, chopped pickles, or perhaps some mint jelly. If red will look best, my favorite garnish is one of the salad sprinkles, such as McCormick's Salad Supreme. It's far more flavorful than just paprika. Sometimes some sliced, stuffed olives or a mound of chopped black olives looks good. Freshly grated cheese is good on hot foods or salads. So is minced onion.

Croutons come in handy for trimming soups and salads, and for use as a casserole topping. French-fried onion rings from a can make a good topping, too; so do nuts. Add such toppings last—they'll get soggy if cooked with the casserole unless you are baking in a conventional oven.

One of my favorite secret weapons is chopped Heath candy bars. They're good on cakes, puddings, canned fruit. An easy chocolate trim is to shave a chocolate bar with a potato peeler. It makes attractive curls. Granola can be sprinkled on canned desserts, too.

For really special occasions when you are trying to make a canned ham or roast look extra festive, peel an onion and stand it firmly on the cutting board. Slice through but not quite to the bottom, in many wedges. Then soak for several hours in a roomy jar of water to which you've added several drops of food coloring. The onion will absorb the color and spread until it looks like a chrysanthemum. Use one or two on the meat platter. Afterwards they can always be eaten as onions in some cooked food where the color won't show.

Throughout the book in places where they are appropriate, you'll find recipes for mock hollandaise sauce (in Chapter 4, "Breakfasts"), various sweet sauces for cakes and puddings (in Chapter 14, "Desserts"), cream sauce (page 61), and other sauces. Quick sauces can also be made from commercial mixes (béarnaise, hollandaise, white sauce, and cheese sauce all come in packets). Lightly thinned cream soups are saucy, and so are full-strength, semi-condensed Soup for One and instant-soup packets made with about half the usual water. All such soups, though, are very salty even when made full strength so they'll be exceedingly salty when concentrated

You'll also find a number of ready-made sauces in cans and jars in the supermarket. Gravies are usually found with canned meats, and sauces are found in the gourmet department as well as on regular food shelves. To heat, just place the opened can or jar in a shallow pan of water and heat. From-scratch sauces can be made ahead and kept hot in vacuum bottles.

Set aside one small corner of a locker for special, colorful, and flavorful foods that can be used as garnishes and trims. These could include tiny jars of maraschino cherries, chopped black olives, stuffed olives, pickled onions, dried chives, button mushrooms, candied fruit, slivered almonds, and jellies.

10. SOUPS

Nothing is more healing after a cold, rough day than a bowl of hot and hearty soup. These recipes were chosen because in most cases they are simplified over multi-step, old-fashioned recipes that take all day, yet they all have homemade flavor, plenty of body, and a touch of class.

One comment about preparation. Some of my recipes call for placing something in the bowl before adding the soup. It's an idea I picked up in Germany where we were once served bowls containing nothing but an egg yolk sprinkled with parsley. The waiter came around with a sort of broth which he whipped into the yolk with great flourish. I find that it is often simpler to apportion garnishes and certain ingredients this way and it saves scraping around in the bottom of the kettle, trying to make sure everyone gets an even portion.

Hot Soups

Cheesy Corn Chowder

4 dabs butter (see Glossary)
1 cup shredded sharp cheese
1 large potato, diced
1 large onion, diced
1 small can diced carrots
2 cups water
1 can tuna (6½ to 7 ounces)
a pinch of thyme
1 can (8 ounces) cream-style corn
1 large can (13 ounces) evaporated milk

Set out four roomy soup bowls and place a dab of butter and a quarter-cup of grated cheese in each one. Boil the vegetables in the water until all are tender, then stir in tuna, corn, and thyme. Heat just to boiling, then remove the pan from the heat and add the evaporated milk. Heat through but take care not to boil it. Ladle into bowls.

Pumpkin Soup

This recipe originated with Judy Olsen aboard the charter yacht *Foxy Lady* out of St. Thomas. In the West Indies, "pumpkin" is what we call squash. Use fresh, mashed butternut or acorn squash—both of them keep well aboard—or canned pumpkin. Just make sure you buy straight pumpkin, not pumpkin pie filling.

2 one-pound cans pumpkin or 3 pounds fresh pumpkin
3 cups milk
2 tablespoons butter
2 tablespoons brown sugar

1 teaspoon salt
¼ teaspoon cayenne pepper

Peel, seed, and cube the pumpkin or squash and boil it in a little water until it's soft and mushy. Whisk or mash it smooth. Scald the milk, mix in the butter and seasonings, and add it bit by bit to the pumpkin, stirring all the while to blend smoothly. Reheat but do not boil. Makes six to seven cups soup.

Creamed Vegetable Soup

1 medium onion, finely chopped
2 tablespoons butter
2 tablespoons cornstarch
1 can (14½ ounces) chicken broth
½ teaspoon salt
a dash of pepper
1 small can evaporated milk
1 small can vegetables, drained

Sauté the onion in butter until tender. Make a paste with the cornstarch and a little broth, stirring and thinning to make a smooth mixture, then pour it into the pan with the onion. Cook it over medium heat until it's thickened. Add the vegetables and milk and heat through. Season as follows:

½ teaspoon dried savory with green beans
¼ teaspoon sage with peas
½ teaspoon dill weed with potatoes
½ teaspoon dried basil with diced carrots

Serve in bowls in which you have placed croutons, and garnish with freeze-dried chives.

Chowder (Master Recipe)

Bacon or salt pork, onion, and potatoes are basic to every chowder recipe, and they are items you can have aboard with you at all times. Although bacon is available in cans, the advantage to having some of the cured bacon or salt pork which need no refrigeration (see *bacon* in Glossary) is that you can hack off only a few slices every time you want chowder.

To serve four:

2 or 3 slices bacon or one-by-two-inch square of salt pork
2 or 3 medium potatoes, diced
1 large onion, diced
1 to 2 cups cooked or raw seafood
1 eight-ounce can cream-style corn (optional)
1 large can evaporated milk
salt and pepper to taste
thyme
4 pats butter

Fry out the meat in a roomy kettle, then add the onions to fry them golden in the fat. Add the potatoes and toss them around in the hot fat to coat them, then cover with water and boil until the vegetables are tender. Add the seafood and canned corn, heat thoroughly. Remove from heat and add the canned milk, then reheat if necessary but do not boil. Set out four bowls and place a pat of butter in each. Sprinkle the butter with a fine dusting of thyme, then ladle in the hot chowder.

Variations: add curry powder to taste, dried celery or bell pepper if you have it, a tablespoon or two of ketchup or tomato paste, or add a small can of mixed vegetables. For a tomato-based chowder, proceed as above but use canned tomatoes for all the liquid, and omit the evaporated milk; do not use cream-style corn. If a thinner chowder is desired, add a can of ready-to-serve (not concentrated) chicken or beef bouillon.

Minute Minestrone

1 can condensed minestrone soup
1 can zucchini in tomato sauce
1 can condensed bean soup
1 cup cabbage, in long shreds
3 soup-cans water
½ cup macaroni or broken spaghetti
grated cheese

Combine all the ingredients except the cheese and pasta, and bring to a boil. Add the pasta and simmer the soup until the pasta is tender. Ladle it into bowls and pass the grated cheese. This makes almost five cups soup.

Variation: dice two slices bacon and one large onion, and fry them until the bacon is crisp. Then add soups and proceed as above.

Cold Soups

These recipes were chosen because, unlike so many cold soups, they require no blender or fresh cream. You can make your own yogurt and have it on hand always. If, however, your homemade yogurt is very thick, as some prefer it, thin these soups with a little reconstituted nonfat dry milk.

Carrot Cocktail

1 can (12 ounces) carrot juice
2 cups yogurt
½ teaspoon dill weed
½ teaspoon salt
a dash of Tabasco

Shake all ingredients briskly in a large, lidded jar, pour into dishes or mugs, and serve at once.

Sprouts Soup

1 can condensed beef broth
1 soup-can water
½ cup alfalfa sprouts
1 tablespoon dried onion
8 water chestnuts, sliced
soy sauce

Combine the broth, water, sprouts, and onion and let them stand a few hours for flavors to blend and onion to soften. Slice two water chestnuts thinly into each bowl, then ladle the broth over them. Pass the soy sauce. Serves two or three.

Blueberry Soup

1 can blueberry pie filling
5 cups yogurt
a dash of salt
¼ teaspoon cinnamon

Mix everything together, reserving a half-cup of the yogurt for a garnish. Makes five or six servings.

Red Snapper

1 can condensed tomato soup
1 can (5½ ounces) cranberry juice cocktail
½ soup-can water
yogurt

Mix the top three ingredients, divide into two or three bowls, and float a dollop of yogurt on each.

Peanut Butter Soup

2 cups yogurt
½ cup peanut butter
1 twelve-ounce can (about 2 cups) tomato juice
1 small sweet onion, grated
½ teaspoon seasoned salt
dill weed

Use a whisk to combine the yogurt and peanut butter until smooth, then whisk in the tomato juice, onion, and salt. Garnish with dill weed. Makes four one-cup servings.

Sweet Lemon Soup

2 eggs
⅓ cup sugar
2 tablespoons lemon juice
1 teaspoon grated lemon rind
4 cups yogurt

Whisk eggs and sugar until they're light and fluffy, then whisk in the remaining ingredients. Makes about four and a half cups soup.

Galley Tips: Soups
Wash an old soy sauce bottle, fill it with sherry, and replace the plastic shaker insert. Pass it at the table so the sherry can be dashed into soups and stews to individual taste.

If any homemade soup or stew turns out too thin, thicken it by sprinkling it with instant potato flakes. Stir constantly. This thickener will not lump.

Butter some scraps of dried bread, brown them in a skillet, and float them in bowls of soup.

Add body to canned soups by sprinkling a mashed hard-boiled egg over each serving.

Following package directions, mix up a small batch of instant mashed potatoes and float a mound of them in each bowl of soup.

Thicken and extend canned or packaged soups by making dumplings. Use biscuit mix (see page 218) and enough water to make a very stiff dough. Spoon the dumplings onto boiling soup, cook ten minutes uncovered, then ten minutes covered.

Enrich any clear soup by placing a raw egg or egg yolk in each bowl. Stir in very hot broth, which will cook the egg.

Garnish pea, bean, or lentil soups with paper-thin slices cut from hard sausage.

Place a cube of soft cheese or a tablespoon of Cheez Whiz into each bowl of hot cream soup and stir to marble it.

Lend an interesting essence to clear soups by floating one or two paper-thin slices of lemon in each bowl.

Top each serving of beet soup with a dollop of thick yogurt or sour cream.

Garnish bowls of soup with: popcorn, twisted pretzels, oyster crackers, Chex cereals, or triangles cut from leftover toast.

To make packaged or canned French onion soup even Frenchier, arrange scraps of buttered bread in a heavy skillet, buttered side down. Pile tops with grated cheese. Cover and place over medium flame until bread is browned and cheese melted. Float in soup.

Cut up one or two soft pitted prunes into each bowl before ladling out chicken-vegetable-type soups.

11. STOW-ABOARD SALADS

Variety and texture contrast are the key words in salads that come from the cupboard, and it is in this course of the meal that we face the biggest challenge in living without supermarkets or refrigeration. When you can find local produce, fine. Use it. My purpose here is only to suggest recipes containing foods that are available to you anywhere, no matter how far from a store or how long you have been without ice.

By far the mainstay of our salads is cabbage. Buy fresh, firm heads and remove any plastic wrap or slimy leaves. If possible, buy heads with coarse outer leaves still attached. Stow where cabbage can get good air circulation, and don't remove drying outer leaves unless they get foul. When you use a cabbage, don't cut through the head. Discard inedible leaves, then peel off leaves as needed for the meal. Outer leaves will continue to protect inner ones, whereas if you cut through the head, exposing all layers, all will spoil quickly. Even though some cabbage may go to waste eventually, this method keeps cabbage for at least two months in my galley.

Apples and citrus fruit, bought in season, are excellent keepers. That term "in season," by the way, is a detail that we may forget in this era of long-distance trucking and cold storage, but it is important when you're stowing produce for the long haul. Fresh October apples will be hard and long-lived. Storage apples bought in April or May, then kept at room temperature, will naturally spoil faster.

I wash all such fruit in cool water with a little detergent, then I rinse, dry, and wrap them separately in clean paper towels. They are stowed where they'll get plenty of air and no bruises. The toweling keeps the fruit clean and ready to eat without washing, isolates any that spoil, and can be reused.

Sprouts are the only good source of salad nutrients that you can make fresh as needed. Shop in health-food stores for special sprouting seeds, for instructions that apply to the many different types, and for equipment, if you need it. I sprout mung beans in a plastic dish with holes punched in the lid for easy rinsing and draining each day. Finer seeds, such as alfalfa, need a fine-mesh strainer for daily rinsing.

Some items are always picked green, and can be bought this way before a cruise so they won't ripen until days later. We once bought a half-bushel of completely green tomatoes in Nassau and a half-bushel of mixed red and pink tomatoes. We had juicy red tomatoes for the entire winter. Bananas are always picked green. Try to get them before the store ripens them. Avocado can also be bought hard and unready, then used after it softens.

Many fruits and vegetables can be dried on purpose, and you can find instructions for dehydrating in such books as Farm Journal's *How to Dry Fruits and Vegetables at Home* and *Don Holm's Book of Food Drying, Pickling and Smoke Curing* (Caxton Printers). Lemons and peppers, however, may dry out gradually and unintentionally in the right conditions of temperature and humidity. Don't throw them away. A lemon, even though it's hard and dry, can be soaked in hot water, then squeezed. Wrinkly green pepper, as long as it has not spoiled, can be added to soups and stews.

After cabbage, our most important salad ingredient is sweet onion. I add it to salads made from canned vegetables, to canned potato salad, and even to some fruit combinations. Sometimes for weeks it is the only fresh ingredient left on board, and we bring along as much as we can. Buy fresh, firm, well-dried varieties and stow them where they'll get plenty of air. Garlic, like onion, keeps for months but not everyone can eat it raw.

Nuts and dried fruits can be added to canned fruit to contribute contrast and crunch. Canned, packaged, or fresh coconut, raisins, and little marshmallows are long-lasting ingredients for fruit salads.

To make salads as fresh-tasting, colorful, and varied as possible, it's important to overcome traditional prejudices about combinations. At home we seldom think of putting vegetables other than celery in tuna or potato salad. Yet I've used grated cabbage, diced apple, finely diced cabbage core, nuts, diced sweet onion, pickles, sprouts, and even canned vegetables in them.

The following are recipes you can have any time from supplies carried on board.

 Ambrosia

There are many variations of this southern favorite, some calling for sour cream or whipped cream. Make it in your galley with a combination of canned and fresh fruits and a splash of sauterne if you like.

6 ripe bananas
6 oranges (or 2 cans mandarin oranges)
1 cup grated coconut
1 cup sugar

If you're using canned oranges, drain them very well and save the juice for rum punch. If you're using fresh oranges, peel and dice them and drink any excess juice. Slice the bananas. Toss all the ingredients together lightly and serve topped with yogurt if you like. Note: this is a very good way to use stale coconut that has become too dry; the oranges moisten it.

Sauerkraut Slaw

This recipe appeared in the first *Cooking on the Go* and it's still a favorite with David and Lee Lander who host the charter boat *Sueño* out of St. Thomas.

> **1 large can sauerkraut**
> **2 large onions, diced**
> **1½ cups sugar**
> **½ cup vinegar**
> **garlic salt to taste**

Drain the kraut in a sieve or colander, rinse, and drain it again. Dice and add the onion, and any other fresh vegetables, such as green pepper, you have on hand. Mix the sugar and vinegar with a whisk for two minutes, even though the sugar will not dissolve completely. Pour the sugar mixture over the kraut and let it stand several hours or overnight. The sugar will dissolve. Alternate versions of this recipe call for the addition of one-half to three-quarters cup salad oil, and for heating the oil, vinegar, and sugar together before pouring them over the kraut.

Overnight Slaw

This fresh-cabbage version of Sauerkraut Slaw also improves with waiting. Make it early in the morning to eat with lunch or dinner or, better still, let it steep overnight. It's a recipe of my old camping friend, Wanda Cassil of Urbana, Illinois.

> **1 large head cabbage, shredded**
> **1 onion, chopped**
> **¾ cup sugar**
> **1 cup vinegar**
> **1 cup salad oil**
> **1 teaspoon dry mustard**

Layer the cabbage and onion in a roomy container and

sprinkle them with the sugar. Bring the vinegar and mustard to a boil, add the oil, and pour over the cabbage. Let it stand, overnight if possible.

Carrot–Coconut Salad

1 cup flaked coconut
1 can julienne carrots, drained
¼ cup raisins
1 tablespoon lemon juice
⅓ cup salad dressing

Toss all the ingredients together with any bottled or homemade vinegar-and-oil-type dressing.

Garbanzo Salad

This is a hearty, meaty salad so serve it in small portions as a side dish. Or make it a luncheon main dish with fresh bread and butter.

1 can garbanzo beans
1 small onion, minced
¼ cup vinegar
1 tablespoon dried parsley
2 tablespoons salad oil
1 tiny jar pimentos, chopped

Drain and rinse the garbanzos, then combine with the other ingredients and mix thoroughly.

Barley Salad

This is a very filling, starchy salad to serve as a vegetarian main dish or as a side dish with meat or fish.

1⅓ cups water
1 cup medium pearl barley
¼ teaspoon salt
1 clove garlic
1 cup yogurt
¼ cup salad oil
3 tablespoons vinegar
¼ teaspoon pepper
1 one-pound can peas, drained
6 hard-boiled eggs, cut up
dill weed

Cook the barley according to package directions. Mash the garlic and rub the inside of a roomy bowl, then discard the pulp. Combine the yogurt with the oil, vinegar, and pepper. Fold in the cooled barley, eggs, and peas, and toss together lightly. Sprinkle generously with dill weed.

Chinese Salad

This recipe was given to me by Alice Stapleton aboard *Basa Anderea,* chartering out of St. Thomas. Although she uses fresh celery and green onions, I have included the salad in this section because it can also be made with Spanish or Bermuda onion. It's a main dish for lunch or for a light supper on a hot night.

2 seven-ounce cans medium shrimp
1 can bean sprouts (fresh sprouts if you prefer)
1 eight-ounce can bamboo shoots
1 eight-ounce can water chestnuts
1 medium sweet onion, diced (or about a cup of mixed green pepper, diced celery, and green onion if you have them)
2 dill pickles

Drain all the canned goods well. Many cooks like to rinse shrimp and drain again. Cut up the sprouts, water chestnuts, and bamboo shoots and dice the pickles. Add the other fresh ingredients or onion, and toss with dressing:

¼ to ⅓ cup mayonnaise (or substitute yogurt)
juice of one small lemon
a pinch of thyme
1 teaspoon prepared mustard
salt and pepper to taste

Three-Bean Salad with Creamy Dressing

There are many versions of salads which consist of several types of canned beans. This one from Ann Glenn aboard the trimaran *Encore* in the Virgin Islands has a very interesting dressing using nonfat dry milk.

  1 large can (18 ounces) chickpeas (garbanzo beans)
  1 one-pound can kidney beans
  1 can black beans
  1 cup yogurt
  2 to 4 tablespoons lemon juice
  ⅔ cup nonfat milk powder
  2 tablespoons honey
  ½ teaspoon salt
  ¼ teaspoon curry powder
  ½ teaspoon basil
  1 tablespoon freeze-dried chives (more if you have fresh)
  1 tablespoon dried parsley (3 tablespoons if fresh)

Drain all the beans well and combine them. In a separate bowl, stir the yogurt until it's smooth, then add a paste made from the lemon juice and milk powder. Blend in the honey and herbs. Pour the dressing over the beans, toss gently, and let stand several hours to let flavors permeate the beans. Drain well, or serve with a draining spoon.

Carrot Salad

It is difficult to halve this big salad, because the dressing contains a full can of tomato soup, so save this recipe for company or a dockside potluck supper.

  2 one-pound cans baby carrots
  2 large sweet onions
  1 can condensed tomato soup
  ½ cup sugar
  ¼ cup vinegar
  1 tablespoon prepared mustard

102

Drain the carrots, rinse, and drain again. Slice the onions very thin. Combine the dressing ingredients, then add the vegetables and toss lightly. Cover and let stand a few hours to let flavors blend. Then toss again, drain, and serve.

 Hot Cole Slaw

3 cups coarsely shredded cabbage
4 tablespoons bacon fat or salad oil
2 tablespoons bacon or imitation bacon bits
3 tablespoons vinegar
salt and pepper to taste

Toss all together in a skillet over medium heat until it's heated through and the cabbage is glossy. Do not overcook! Cabbage should remain crisp. Serve warm.

⚓ Red Cabbage Slaw

1 large can (one pound or 12 ounces) julienne beets
3 cups shredded cabbage
up to ¼ cup sugar
1 eight-ounce jar mayonnaise
a dash of nutmeg

Drain the beets well, combine them with the cabbage, and sprinkle lightly with sugar. Let stand 15 minutes or more until sugar forms a glaze. Toss lightly with remaining ingredients and serve at once.

🐚 Beet Curry Salad

This salad begins with versatile canned beets, which I like as a cruising staple because they hold their texture well when canned and because they can be served hot or cold. The recipe comes from Sue Moesly who circumnavigated aboard *Svea* with her husband, Don.

1 one-pound can diced beets
½ cup vinegar
½ cup salad oil
1 sweet onion, thinly sliced or diced
salt, pepper, and curry powder to taste

Combine all ingredients and let stand several hours before serving. Drain well.

🐚 Fiesta Salad

Credit Sue Moesly for this salad, too. A packaged mix adds an interesting twist.

1 package Sloppy Joe mix
1 cup water
¼ cup vinegar
¼ cup salad oil
1 small (eight-ounce) can tomatoes
1 one-pound can whole-kernel corn
1 one-pound can cut green beans
1 small (eight-ounce) can pitted black olives

Combine first four ingredients and pour over the well-drained vegetables. Let stand several hours, then drain and serve.

Your Own Mayonnaise

Shake it up in a glass jar or blend it with a beater. This makes almost a pint of creamy salad dressing for potato or macaroni salad. It will be thinner than the bottled mayonnaise you are used to.

1 tablespoon sugar
½ teaspoon salt
a dash of pepper
½ cup evaporated milk
2½ tablespoons vinegar
1½ cups salad oil

Mix the dry ingredients with the milk, then beat or shake in the vinegar. Let it stand for a few minutes for vinegar to thicken the milk. Then add the oil and shake again.

Cooked Salad Dressing

2 tablespoons cornstarch
1 teaspoon salt
1 teaspoon dry mustard
2 tablespoons sugar
1 egg
¾ cup milk
¼ cup vinegar
2 tablespoons butter

In a heavy saucepan over very low heat, combine the dry ingredients and stir in the egg and milk. Remove from heat. Very gradually add the vinegar, then butter, stirring constantly.

 Hot Bacon Dressing

Similar to the dressings usually used on fresh spinach salad, this one is also good over canned green beans or boiled potatoes.

2 slices bacon, diced
1 small onion, minced
2 tablespoons vinegar
1 teaspoon sugar
½ teaspoon salt
a dash of pepper
½ teaspoon prepared mustard
1 egg

In a small pan, fry out the bacon with the onion until both are well cooked. Stir in all the other ingredients except the egg. Using a small bowl or paper cup, beat the egg with a fork and add a small amount of the bacon mixture. Blend well, then add the egg to the rest of the bacon mixture. Stir over low heat until the dressing is thick and hot, but do not let it boil. Pour over vegetables.

⚓ Low-Cal Yogurt Dressing

This dressing doesn't contain oil, so don't expect it to be as rich as other dressings. Still, it's a low-calorie spicer for canned vegetables or any fresh greens you have found.

1 cup yogurt (not too thick)
2 teaspoons prepared mustard
a pinch of minced onion flakes
1 teaspoon dried parsley
a dash of salt and pepper
a dash of dill weed

Combine all ingredients in a jar and shake to blend. Pour over vegetables.

Creamy Mushroom Dressing

1 can cream of mushroom soup
¼ cup water
¼ cup vinegar
2 tablespoons sugar
1 teaspoon prepared mustard
a dash each of celery seed and dill weed

Combine in a small pan and heat gently, stirring until smooth. Cool and pour over vegetables.

French Dressing

1 packet instant tomato soup
½ cup hot water
¼ cup salad oil
2 tablespoons vinegar
1 or 2 tablespoons grated Parmesan cheese
a dash of garlic salt
½ teaspoon basil
½ teaspoon oregano

Combine the soup and water in a small jar, stir, and let cool. Add the remaining ingredients and shake well. Pour over vegetables.

Galley Tips: Salads

Shop for variety in all aisles of your supermarket for items you can serve as salad courses. Carry tiny jars of pimento for color, water chestnuts for crunch, pickles and olives of every type, chutneys for a change, corn relish, pickled onions, and even nuts. The day comes when you crave them all as a switch from bland, canned foods.

Drain canned green beans well and toss with vinegar and oil dressing. Sprinkle with croutons, bread crumbs, grated cheese, or chopped hard-boiled egg.

Arrange well-drained tinned tomatoes (drink the juice in a vegetable cocktail) in a salad dish and sprinkle with parsley flakes or freeze-dried chives. Dried dill weed also makes an excellent herb for canned vegetable "salads."

Make toothpick-a-bobs with olives, pickle chunks, squares of cheese, pickled onions, croutons, water chestnuts, artichoke hearts, or what have you.

Served canned tomatoes with a sprinkling of salt, sugar, pepper, and grated cheese.

Add sliced, fresh sweet onion to pickled beets or sweet-and-sour cabbage from a jar. Or serve the sweet-and-sour cabbage with real or imitation bacon bits.

Mash whole-cranberry sauce and mix with well-drained mandarin oranges from a can.

If you have no celery to add to potato or macaroni salad, try nuts, apple chunks, sliced water chestnuts, grated fresh cabbage, or finely diced cabbage core.

Sauce well-drained, canned asparagus with vinegar and oil dressing. Garnish with sliced hard-boiled eggs and pimento strips.

Mix corn relish with drained canned corn to serve as a salad.

Marinate well-drained canned baby whole carrots in vinegar and oil dressing. Serve sprinkled with dried parsley or freeze-dried chives.

Soak dried apples overnight, drain, and mix with sweet-and-sour red cabbage from a jar.

Drain any can of fruit and make it into fruit salad by adding cut-up raisins, dates, pitted prunes, nuts, grated coconut, candied cherries, or anything else you can contribute from the shelf to add color and variety. For extra interest, soak dried fruit or raisins in rum or liqueur for an hour before making the salad.

Slice tomato aspic from a can and sprinkle with dill weed or dried parsley.

Sweet red onions last for many weeks. Slice one into paper-thin rings and serve with canned orange or grapefruit sections.

Toss drained canned peas with vinegar and oil dressing, and garnish with quartered hard-boiled egg.

Stock jars of colorful apple rings, pickled pears, and pickled peaches to serve as salads.

Buy dried banana flakes to toss with canned fruits.

Buy fruit salad in a jar or fruit cocktail in a can, then mix with cut-up marshmallows. Marshmallows will keep for weeks if double-wrapped and kept very dry.

Visit a natural foods store before each cruise and stock up on seeds for sprouting. Although mung beans and alfalfa are best known, dozens of other things from wheat to garbanzos can be sprouted for an unending supply of fresh salad vegetables.

Drain a can of artichoke hearts, halve them, drain again, then serve with salad dressing.

Check the gourmet foods section for unusual canned vegetables which can be turned into a substitute salad. Hearts of palm, imported aspics and gels, baby ears of corn, antipastos, and white asparagus are a few of the unusual items which will add variety to meals from your lockers.

Drain canned peach or pear halves well and put together with a ball of chunky peanut butter in the center. Sprinkle completed "whole" fruit with coconut or cookie crumbs and serve as a dessert-salad.

Add a rosy blush and a special tang to canned applesauce by stirring in a teaspoon or two of red or orange sweetened drink mix.

12. BREADS

All of these recipes can be baked atop the stove according to one of the methods described on pages 15 to 18.

Ship's Bread

Since this recipe first appeared in the original *Cooking on the Go* it has been shared and printed widely. It is still the cruising sailor's seagoing staff of life.

> 1½ cups lukewarm water (or 1 cup water plus ½ cup sea water)
> 1 packet (1 tablespoon) dry yeast
> 2 teaspoons salt (if you are not using sea water)
> 1 tablespoon sugar or honey
> 4 cups flour (see below)
> 2 tablespoons cornmeal
> shortening for pan

In this recipe, as much as half the flour measure can be made up of whole wheat or other flours and up to four tablespoons soy flour. One-third cup of nonfat dry milk can also be added to the flour measure if you like. Combine the yeast, water, salt, and sugar and let the mixture stand without stirring. After about five minutes, the yeast will have dissolved. Stir and knead in flour. Let the dough rise in a warm place about 90 minutes or until it has doubled in bulk. Stir down and turn into a pressure cooker which has been greased and coated with cornmeal. Let the dough rise until it has again doubled in bulk, and bake over a medium flame. Cooking times vary according to the size and type of pressure cooker, type of fuel, and type of stove. This recipe takes 45 minutes to bake over a medium kerosene Primus burner, with an asbestos shield, in a four-quart, old-style (heavy) aluminum pressure cooker.

🐚 English Muffins

1 cup warm water
1 package (1 tablespoon) dry yeast
1 teaspoon sugar
2 teaspoons salt
¼ cup shortening
3 cups flour

Sprinkle yeast over the water in a roomy bowl, and mix in the remaining ingredients. Flour may be all white, or a mixture of white flour with up to one cup whole-wheat flour. On a floured cloth or paper towel, roll out the dough to about one third of an inch and cut into circles. Arrange these on waxed paper which has been sprinkled with cornmeal, and allow them to rise until doubled. Bake on a preheated griddle over a medium flame until the muffins are browned on both sides. To serve, split and toast.

Some muffin variations:

- For sweeter muffins, add two tablespoons honey or brown sugar.
- Add raisins, chopped nuts, or any soft dried fruit.
- Add one tablespoon orange drink mix powder.
- Make muffins with half rye, half white flour, and add caraway seeds plus a pinch of grated orange peel.

- Knead in a half-cup of sliced onion, sautéed until yellow.
- Knead in one cup grated cheese.
- Add a half-cup mashed sweet potatoes plus a half-teaspoon vanilla and a little grated orange peel.

 ## Swedish Steamed Rye

1 packet (1 tablespoon) dry yeast
1¼ cups lukewarm water
1 teaspoon salt (or use ½ cup sea water as part of water measure)
¾ cup molasses
4 cups rye flour
1 cup white flour

Put the warm water in a bowl and sprinkle with yeast. Let it stand five minutes, then add salt, molasses, and rye flour. Mix well, then add the remaining flour. Knead the dough on a floured board or towel until smooth. Divide it into three or four portions and place them in greased tin cans that will fit into your pressure cooker. Each can should be only half full. Let the dough rise in a warm place until it has almost doubled in bulk, cover each can with foil, and place it on a rack in the pressure cooker with water coming about two-thirds up the side of the can. (Don't use sea water for steaming; it may clog the pressure regulator.) Bring to a boil and steam, letting the steam escape for 20 minutes. Then cook under ten pounds pressure for 40 minutes. Cool. Remove the can bottoms with a can opener, loosen the loaves around the edges, and push out the bread. Cut each loaf into four lengthwise wedges. Then slice thinly and serve with butter.

Baking Powder and Baking Soda

🥜 Beer Bread

This amazingly yeasty bread is the easiest you've ever made. It slices surprisingly well, and holds together for sandwich use.

> 3 cups self-rising flour (or 3 cups flour, 3 teaspoons baking
> powder, and 1 teaspoon salt)
> 1 to 3 tablespoons sugar
> 1 can beer
> melted butter (optional)

Mix together all the ingredients except the butter, and turn into a greased and cornmeal-coated pressure cooker. Bake by the direct method until the bread tests done with a toothpick. Turn it out of the pan and drizzle it with melted butter. For oven baking, use a nine-by-five-by-three-inch loaf pan and bake at 375° for about 35 minutes.

Johnnycake

> 1 cup cornmeal
> 1 cup flour
> ½ teaspoon salt
> 1 cup milk
> 4 teaspoons baking powder
> 1 egg
> ¼ cup oil
> ¼ cup sugar

Combine all the ingredients in a heavy-duty plastic bag and squeeze it to mix. Strip the batter from the bag into a pan and bake by the direct or indirect method.

114

Double Cornbread

This is a heavier, custardlike bread best eaten with a fork.

2 tablespoons butter
3 eggs
½ cup cornmeal
½ cup flour
2 teaspoons baking powder
2 tablespoons sugar
1 one-pound can cream-style corn
½ teaspoon salt
sliced cheese (optional)

Melt the butter in a heavy skillet and combine the remaining ingredients, using a plastic bag as described above. Bake by the direct or indirect method until the bread is springy to the touch. Top with sliced cheese if desired, and cover for a minute or two until the cheese melts. Cut into wedges and serve hot with butter.

 ## Christmas Bread

2 cups flour
1½ teaspoons baking powder
½ teaspoon baking soda
¾ cup sugar
1 teaspoon salt
1 one-pound can whole cranberry sauce
1 teaspoon grated orange peel
½ cup chopped nuts
¾ cup orange juice or orange drink

Mix the dry ingredients, then mash in the cranberries with a fork. Add the remaining ingredients just until blended. Bake in a loaf pan at 350° or by any indirect method. Cool, then wrap in foil or plastic. To serve, slice and butter.

🐚 Banana Bread

All of us who have bought bananas by the stalk when cruising know how desperate things get when all the bananas ripen at once. Start early by serving cooked green bananas as a vegetable. Then enjoy the ready-to-eat, ripe bananas. Finally, when the fruit is getting overripe, make banana bread and slather slices of it with—not butter, but mashed bananas!

3 or 4 bananas
⅓ cup butter
⅔ cup sugar
2 eggs
3 tablespoons sour milk
1 teaspoon baking powder
1 teaspoon salt
2 cups flour
½ teaspoon baking soda

In a roomy bowl, mash the bananas to a smooth paste with a fork, then use the fork or your hands to work in the fat, eggs, sugar, and milk. If you don't have sour milk, sour any sweet milk (reconstituted dry, diluted canned, fresh) with a splash of vinegar. Add the remaining ingredients and mix well. For oven baking, use a square or loaf pan at 350° or bake by the indirect method. This recipe fills three #303 (16-ounce) tins two-thirds full. Banana bread is delicious warm, cold, or buttered and fried.

Steamboat Bread

2 cups mixed flours (white, whole wheat, cornmeal, rye)
2½ teaspoons baking powder
½ teaspoon salt
2 tablespoons honey or molasses
1 cup milk
1 cup raisins or any ready-to-eat dried fruit

Blend the dry ingredients and stir in the milk, fruit, and honey or molasses. Mix well. Turn the batter into one large can or several smaller cans that fit into your pressure cooker. Soda cans work especially well. Fill the cans no more than two-thirds full. Top each one with foil and place on a rack in the pressure cooker. Add enough water to reach two-thirds of the way up the sides of the cans. Boil, letting steam escape, for 20 minutes. Then raise the pressure to ten pounds and cook 25 minutes more.

Quick Biscuits

You save time and mess with this recipe because there is no shortening to cut in.

1½ cups flour
1½ teaspoons baking powder
¼ teaspoon baking soda
½ teaspoon salt
½ cup milk
½ teaspoon vinegar
¼ cup salad oil

Mix all the dry ingredients, then add the remaining ingredients and blend with a fork just until mixed. Turn the batter out onto a floured cloth or paper towel, knead lightly, flatten with your hands, and cut into squares or circles. Place them in a cold, lightly greased, heavy aluminum skillet, cover, and bake two or three minutes. Turn them over and bake two or three minutes more. Continue baking, covered, and turning until dough is done throughout and biscuits are nicely browned outside.

🐚 Scottish Oat Biscuits

This makes a very large amount of nutty, coarsely textured, whole-grain cakes that are delicious served with butter and jam. Halve the recipe for a smaller crew.

3 cups rolled oats
3 cups flour
1 cup sugar
2 teaspoons salt
1 teaspoon soda
1½ cups shortening
½ cup cold water

Cut the shortening into a mixture of the dry ingredients. Add water and mix well. Turn out onto a floured cloth and knead lightly, just to make the dough workable. Roll or pat out about a half-inch thick and cut into squares or circles. Place these on a cold, lightly greased, heavy aluminum skillet, cover, and bake over medium heat until the biscuits begin to brown. Turn and bake on the other sides until browned, then turn again and continue baking until the dough is cooked throughout. These oat biscuits taste best when served warm.

⚓ Onion Snack Bread

4 medium onions, sliced
2 tablespoons butter
1¼ cups flour
1 teaspoon baking powder
½ teaspoon salt
¼ cup Parmesan cheese
3 tablespoons shortening
½ cup milk
½ cup grated cheddar

Fry the onions in butter until soft and remove them from the skillet. Stir together the flour, baking powder, salt, and Parmesan, cut in the fat, and blend in the milk. Spread the batter into a well-greased heavy skillet. Sprinkle with grated cheddar and top with cooked onions. Cover tightly and bake over a low flame until the edges are lightly browned. Cool slightly and cut into wedges. This is a tasty snack warm or cold.

Pennsylvania Dutch Cheese Bread

½ cup shortening, margarine, or butter
4 cups flour
2 tablespoons sugar
3 teaspoons baking powder
4 cups grated medium cheese (American, cheddar, jack)
1 teaspoon dill weed
2 eggs
2 cups milk

Cut the butter into the dry ingredients until the mixture looks like dry oatmeal. Stir in the cheese and dill. Beat the eggs and milk together, then add all at once, stirring just enough to set the mixture. Bake 35 to 40 minutes using the direct pressure-cooker method. For oven baking, this makes one very large loaf or two small ones. If your pressure cooker is smaller than six quarts, halve the recipe.

Squash Bread

2 cups flour
2 teaspoons baking powder
½ teaspoon salt
¼ teaspoon baking soda
1 cup sugar
2 eggs
1 cup mashed squash, pumpkin or sweet potato
¼ cup oil

Mix the ingredients in two bowls or plastic bags, the wet ingredients in one bag, the dry ones in another. Combine, then bake by any direct or indirect method.

Chappatis

A small skillet is ideal for making this Indian flat bread, but you can also use a crepe pan if you have one.

1½ cups whole-wheat flour
¾ cup white flour
a pinch of salt
1 tablespoon plus 1 teaspoon oil
1¼ cups water

Combine the dry ingredients, add the oil, and make a well in the center. Pour in the water and mix to make a soft dough. Add more water if needed to make a smooth, kneadable dough. Knead for five minutes. Divide into 12 portions, roll each into a ball, and pat each of these into a thin pancake. Cover with a damp towel to keep them moist as you work. Preheat a dry skillet over a medium flame and fry the chappatis one at a time, for a few minutes on each side. The bread will puff up and brown unevenly. Serve them at once.

Yogurt Crackers

2¾ cups flour
a pinch of salt
¼ teaspoon baking soda
½ cup mayonnaise
1 cup yogurt

Mix all the ingredients well and form a ball. Cut it in half, in quarters, and in sixteenths, then form each piece into a small ball. Roll each into a thin circle and bake on both sides on a hot, ungreased griddle. Sprinkle them with salt and cool on racks.

Irish Soda Bread

The beauty of this bread is that, even though it is a quick, no-yeast recipe, the bread slices well, toasts, and holds together in sandwiches, unlike many baking-powder breads, which have too fine a crumb to be handled easily.

4 cups flour
3 tablespoons sugar
¾ teaspoon baking soda
1 tablespoon baking powder
6 tablespoons butter or margarine
2 eggs
1½ cups sour milk

Mix the dry ingredients and cut in the fat. Again, if you don't have sour milk, sour any sweet milk (reconstituted dry, diluted canned, fresh) with a splash of vinegar. Beat the eggs and milk and stir this into the dry mixture. Turn out onto a floured linen or paper towel and knead ten strokes, no more. Traditional Irish recipes call for the addition of one and a half cups raisins to this recipe. Turn into a greased, cornmeal-coated pressure cooker for baking by direct method for about 45 minutes. Cut a cross into the top before baking, to aid in even rising.

🐚 Peanut Butter Bread

1¾ cups flour, part whole wheat if desired
⅓ cup sugar
1 tablespoon baking powder
½ teaspoon salt
1 cup smooth or chunky peanut butter
1 egg
1 cup milk

Mix the dry ingredients and cut in the peanut butter with a pastry blender or with two knives used scissors-fashion. Beat the egg into the milk and stir this into the dry mixture just until it's evenly wet, no more. Use the direct baking method. Cool the bread, wrap it, and let it "age" several hours or overnight for easier slicing.

Bread Spreads

Tinned margarines and butters are sold in many parts of the world, although not commonly in North America. In the United States, you may find tinned, imported butter in gourmet shops. Reserve food outlets (look in the Yellow Pages under "Foods–Dehydrated" or write Family Reserve Foods, 710 S.E. 17th Street, Causeway, Ft. Lauderdale FL 33316) carry canned, powdered butter, which can be reconstituted with water. You can also carry fresh margarine or butter for long periods, depending on the temperature. Even in the warm Bahamas, mine keeps for as long as six weeks. Buy regular margarine, not the whipped or soft types, and press it into sterilized plastic tubs, then lid tightly. The taste and texture will remain fresh if you can keep the butter and margarine from melting, so keep them away from the stove, engine heat, or direct sun.

For a change, try spreading breads with other things, too:

apple or prune butter, peanut butter, mashed bananas, honey or a honey-butter mixture, preserves, soft cheese, or one of the following recipes.

 ## Date Butter

½ cup dates, pitted and cut up
¼ cup water
a dash of salt
a squirt of lemon juice if you have it
½ cup butter or margarine

Cook the dates with water, lemon juice, and salt until the mixture is thick. Remove from heat and mix in the butter or margarine. After the fat has melted, pour the mixture into a small crock or bowl and let cool until it firms.

Praline Topping

¼ cup brown sugar
¼ cup butter or margarine
finely chopped pecans

No amount is given here for pecans but the mixture can hold up to about a cup, depending on how nutty—and costly—you want the spread to be. Mix all ingredients together, and spread on hot toast.

Quick Lemon Curd

1 lemon
1 can lemon pie filling
1 package powdered pectin (found with canning supplies)
1¼ cups sugar

Cut the yellow part only of the lemon rind into small strips, simmer in water for ten minutes, drain, and cool. Stir the pectin into the pie filling, bring to a rolling boil for one minute, add sugar, and bring to the boil again. Stir in the peels and pour into scalded jar(s). Allow to cool, then use it as you would jelly or jam. Finish it off within a couple of days. To preserve the curd longer than that, make a double batch and, while it is still boiling-hot, pour into sterilized jars and seal, using standard jelly-making practice.

Sourdough

Through the ages, travelers have been intrigued with sourdough as a continuing source of leaven and as a tangy, almost fruity taste which was welcome on the trail when no fresh foods were available. However, sourdough presents special problems on boats. As a living culture, the starter must be allowed to "breathe," which means that you have to stow it in a loose-lidded container yet keep it from spilling. Because a metal container could interact with the acids in the culture, it's best to use crockery or glass, yet these are breakable. Pioneers used small wooden buckets for their sourdough because, even if the starter spilled, enough spores were usually caught in the pores of the wood to get the culture started again. But such containers are difficult to find today.

Sourdough starter is a living yeast which must be fed regularly, protected from extreme heat and cold, and covered against unwanted organisms. All this is a tall order on a boat, especially when you have no refrigeration.

As I began my reading on sourdough, I had two special goals in mind. Even though almost all modern recipes specify the addition of new yeast with each baking, I knew that sourdough itself could be used as a replacement for costly, perishable yeast. Second, I had to be able to manage the starter without refrigeration, even though all modern recipes recommend keeping the starter cold after its initial development. I had to start from square one, because all my old-time recipes from before the days of refrigeration were developed by pioneers in Alaska and other cool climates—and we were in the tropics.

Maintaining cultured foods is a skill which is passed on from person to person, and its management evolves in each area according to the temperatures and organisms available. If you can get firsthand instructions, and a cup of starter, from someone who has been using sourdough with success and without refrigeration for a long time, take it gladly. There are many right ways to make Boston baked beans, jerky, and other traditional foods. I know only that my sourdough method works for me, here.

Traditional sourdoughs were started from flour plus milk or potato water which gathered natural yeasts from the air and propagated them. My own culture was started with commercial yeast, which I recommend. In a galley where a lot of bread baking over the years has filled the air with yeast spores, it's likely that you can get the starter going without commercial yeast. In a new boat, though, it's possible that a starter just won't start and costly ingredients will be wasted. I've included three recipes for starter, one with yeast and two without, so you'll have a way to create a new starter if yours becomes inactive and you are caught without any yeast aboard. The former is more reliable, but the latter are more authentic and are worth a try.

Two methods can be used to keep sourdough starter inactive but alive for long-term storage. It can be dried on a saucer in the sun, or commercially dried starters can be purchased (try a health-food store). Or you can add a lot of flour to some of the starter to make a very dry ball, wrap it in clean linen, and bury it in the flour sack. With luck, you'll be able to reactivate dried starter by adding flour and warm water months later.

Occasionally, mold will form on sourdough and in many cases this is just another friendly growth which contributes to the interest and taste of the baked product. To keep unwanted freeloaders out of the starter, transfer it every once in a while to a clean, scalded bowl while you scrub and scald the starter crock. When stirring new flour into the starter, use a well-scalded wooden spoon. If the mixture turns blue or green, many authorities recommend throwing it out but a pink or orange mold is said to be harmless.

In keeping any sourdough alive week after week without refrigeration and in the moist heat of the tropics, I feed it every three days. To replenish the starter, just add an amount of flour equal to that of the starter you have used, an equivalent amount of warm water, and stir. For instance, if you have used a cup of starter, add a cup each of flour and warm water.

Be sure to replenish the starter after using every recipe given here. Starter that is not fed will starve and lose its oomph.

If you want to increase the starter, to give some to a friend, or to make larger batches of baked foods, add an extra cup of flour and one of warm water. Just don't add more than one cup each of flour and water at a time for each cup of sourdough, and don't try to increase it more often than every two or three days.

There is a limit to how much bread and pastry the two of us can eat, but by using a variety of sourdough recipes for bread and pancakes, and by occasionally giving away starter or a loaf of bread, I manage to keep the starter active. It will be less a problem for boats with larger crews, for boats which can refrigerate the starter, and for sailors whose appetites for starches are lustier than ours.

Sourdough Starter #1 (with yeast)

2 packages dry yeast
2 teaspoons sugar
2 cups warm water
4 cups flour (white flour works best for sourdough starters)

Mix all the ingredients into a smooth batter, and place in a crockery or glass bowl. Keep it in a warm place for at least two days before using it for the first time. Store it in a loose-lidded crock.

Sourdough Starter #2 (no yeast)

4 cups flour
2 teaspoons salt
2 tablespoons sugar
3 cups water in which potatoes have been boiled

Beat all ingredients to a smooth batter in a glass or crockery bowl that has room for the batter to expand. Cover it with a clean dish towel and let it stand in a warm place for about a day and a half. Transfer the batter to a scalded crock or jar. Cover with a loose top which will allow the starter to breathe, and keep it at room temperature.

Sourdough Starter #3 (no yeast)

2 cups warm milk
2 cups flour
3 tablespoons yogurt

Warm a roomy glass, hard plastic, or ceramic bowl with hot water and dry it. Stir the yogurt into one cup warmed milk, cover it, and keep in a warm place overnight. You will then have a curd the consistency of yogurt, perhaps with a layer of liquid on top. If that liquid is pink at this point, discard the starter and try again after scalding all the equipment. After you get an acceptable yogurt culture, stir in one cup of the flour. Cover this and let it stand in a warm place (summertime room temperature) until it is frothy and sour. This usually takes anywhere from two to five days. A liquid usually rises to the top; if it's pink, discard all but one-quarter cup of the starter you now have. If it is not pink, proceed using all the starter. In each case, stir one cup each warm milk and flour into the starter and let it stand in a warm place until it is bubbling (about two days). You may now use the starter or double it.

Sourdough Bread

Although most modern recipes call for the addition of new yeast to each sourdough baking, this one relies solely on the sourdough for its rising. It can be mixed the night before and baked in the morning, or mixed just after breakfast to be ready for supper. For me, this recipe works best with white flour and no more than a half-cup of other flours.

4 cups flour
1 cup sourdough starter
1 cup warm water
1½ teaspoons salt
¼ teaspoon baking soda

Place the flour in a large mixing bowl (glass or plastic, not metal), make a well in the center, and add the water and starter. Mix well, stirring in salt. Knead well, adding more flour if necessary and turn into a clean, scalded bowl. Cover with plastic wrap and let it stand eight hours or overnight in a warm (room temperature) place. Turn the dough onto a floured board, sprinkle with the soda, and knead thoroughly. Shape it into a loaf and turn it into a loaf pan or prepared pressure cooker. Let it rise 30 minutes; it will rise further during baking. Using a sharp knife, cut a shallow "X" across the round loaf or a line down the center of a rectangular loaf. This helps prevent uneven cracking during baking. Bake the loaf in a hot oven, or according to the pressure-cooker direct method, for 45 minutes.

⚓ Sourdough Crepes

¾ cup starter
1 cup warm water
1¼ cups flour
2 eggs
3 tablespoons oil
½ teaspoon salt
½ teaspoon baking soda
oil for cooking

Stir together the starter, water, and flour in a roomy bowl. Cover the batter with a clean dish towel and let it stand overnight. (If you are making the crepes for dinner, start the batter first thing in the morning.) Beat in the eggs, oil, salt, and baking soda, cover the bowl, and let stand 15 minutes. Cook the crepes one at a time in a lightly oiled crepe pan or small skillet, browning them on both sides. To serve the crepes as pancakes, stack them, or use them to wrap main dish or dessert fillings.

🐶 Same-Day Sourdough Pancakes

2 tablespoons salad oil
1 tablespoon sugar or honey
a pinch of salt
½ teaspoon baking soda
1 egg
1½ cups sourdough starter

Traditional sourdough pancakes begin the night before, but this quicker method has the same delicious tang. It has the added advantage of using starter without the addition of more flour, so it's a good way to deplete a starter that is getting too large. Using a non-metal bowl, beat all the ingredients together and let stand ten minutes. Bake on a hot griddle.

🐚 Sourdough Sand Dollars

These unusual corn pancakes keep your sourdough cycling, and they are a toothsome change from wheat cakes.

1 cup cornmeal
1 cup milk
1 egg
2 tablespoons honey or sugar
½ cup sourdough starter
2 tablespoons oil
½ teaspoon salt
¼ teaspoon baking soda
½ teaspoon baking powder

Mix the cornmeal and milk and let this stand for about ten minutes. Blend in the other ingredients and fry the batter on a hot griddle as for pancakes. Serve with syrup or honey. Replenish the starter with a half-cup flour and a half-cup warm water.

🔦 Same-Day Sourdough Sweet Rolls

2 cups or more flour
2 teaspoons baking powder
1 teaspoon salt
½ teaspoon baking soda
¾ cup sourdough starter
⅔ cup sour milk or yogurt
½ cup sugar
2 teaspoons cinnamon
1 tablespoon grated orange peel if you have it
1 tablespoon oil
3 tablespoons melted butter

Combine the flour, starter, and sour milk, and knead on a well-floured board, adding more flour if necessary, until well mixed. Do not over-knead; about 15 turns should be enough.

(While yeast doughs improve with kneading, over-kneading makes baking-soda doughs tougher.) Roll the dough into a rectangle as thin as you can comfortably make it (about a quarter-inch) and sprinkle it with the cinnamon, sugar, and orange peel. Add some chopped nuts if you like, then pour the melted butter over all. Roll up the dough, jelly-roll fashion, slice it into 12 equal slices and arrange them in a well-greased baking tin. Brush the surface of the dough with oil. Preheat your oven or stovetop oven very hot, and bake about 25 minutes or until the rolls are browned. If your stovetop oven is not capable of quick, hot temperatures, take care not to over-bake the rolls while waiting in vain for them to brown. This recipe will brown and bake as specified in a preheated aluminum Dutch oven atop a kerosene Primus burner on high heat.

An alternate baking method is pressure-cooker direct, after greasing the cooker and coating it with cornmeal. Use a low flame, as for bread. Do not, however, slice the roll before baking because the sugar in the cinnamon mixture may carbonize on the pan bottom. Roll the dough into a ring, pinch the edges well so no sugar will leak out, and bake about 30 to 45 minutes in the pressure cooker.

Some points about sourdough:

- If you can keep the starter in a refrigerator, you can feed it as infrequently as every two months.

- Young starters may not have as much leavening power as more mature ones. At first, use yeast plus starter, or make quick breads and pancakes which use additional rising agents such as baking soda.

- To test starter that you fear is no longer active, mix a quarter-cup starter with a half-cup each warm water and flour. Cover and let stand in a warm spot, watching it closely for bubbling. If it bubbles in four to eight hours, you know the culture is alive and well. Add this mixture to the starter.

- Starter can be frozen but should be defrosted and replenished four times a year.
- Sourdough contains a living culture that causes it to bubble and swell. Any time you are working with starter or sourdough, use containers large enough to allow for expansion. Even though the starter may bubble up only briefly and then quiet down, it needs room to do so.
- If it's time to feed your starter and you simply don't need any type of bread, use up to a half-cup starter in place of the milk measurement in a cake recipe that calls for buttermilk or sour milk. Then replace the half-cup starter with a half-cup each of flour and warm water, and you're set for another three days. The rest of the liquid used in the cake can be sweet milk because the sourdough provides the acid needed for proper rising.

13. SEAFOOD (CANNED)

One of the best things about galley cooking is that we learn to look at recipes not as commandments carved in stone, but as starting points after which we "make do" according to the weather, our supplies, and our galley equipment. Most of the recipes here can also be used with fresh fish, which is discussed in a different chapter, or with boneless, canned chicken or ham. Also, be sure to check the "Main Dishes" chapter for recipes where you can substitute tuna or salmon.

Stir-Fried Tuna Crisp

2 cans (a total of about 14 ounces) tuna
3 tablespoons oil
1 clove garlic, minced
1 medium onion, sliced
1 small cabbage
2 tablespoons cornstarch
1 cup water
scant teaspoon granular bouillon
1 cup water

Drain the tuna and, if it is packed in oil, use the oil as part or all of the oil measure. Heat the oil in a skillet or wok with the garlic until the garlic sizzles, then add the onion and coarsely cut-up cabbage and stir-fry over high heat. Add the tuna. Make a thick paste with the cornstarch and some of the water, then add the bouillon and remaining water. (If you have only cube bouillon, dissolve it in water first. I prefer granular bouillon for all cruising recipes.) Stir the cornstarch mixture into the tuna mixture. Heat, stirring, until the sauce has cleared and thickened. Serve over rice.

 Tuna Pie

> **2 cups flour**
> **⅔ cup margarine**
> **1 teaspoon salt**
> **water**
> **1 recipe Tuna Crisp (see preceding recipe)**

Cut the margarine into the flour and salt, using two knives held scissors-fashion, or a pastry blender. Toss with just enough water to make the dough form a ball. Divide into two balls. Roll out one into a circle to fit a pie pan which will fit into your stovetop oven. Fill the crust with the tuna mixture and top it with the second ball of dough, rolled out to fit. Seal the edges by moistening very lightly with fingertips dipped in water. This helps bind the top crust to the bottom crust. Flute the edges. Bake by indirect Dutch oven method over the highest heat until the crust browns. Margarine is specified in this recipe because it helps the crust to brown better than shortening does.

Main-Dish Tuna Salad

> **1 seven-ounce can tuna**
> **1 one-pound can white beans**
> **1 small sweet onion, finely diced**
> **juice of half a lemon**
> **salt and pepper to taste**

Drain the beans and tuna, and toss all ingredients thoroughly. This makes a quick and easy cold supper when served with crusty bread and stewed tomatoes.

Codfish Balls

Use your own salted, dried fish or buy commercial salt fish. By deep-frying these little cakes, you add a unique taste and new texture contrast.

> 1 cup salt fish, soaked, drained, and shredded
> 2 cups prepared mashed potatoes
> 1 egg
> salt and pepper to taste

Combine all the ingredients, using salt sparingly if at all because of the salt in the fish. Form into cakes, gently dredge in flour, and fry in hot fat.

Spaghetti in Clam Sauce

> 1 eight-ounce box spaghetti
> 2 cans minced clams, drained (add juice to cooking water)
> ½ cup butter
> grated Parmesan cheese
> 1 tablespoon parsley flakes
> 1 teaspoon garlic salt

Cook the spaghetti until it is just tender. While the spaghetti is cooking, melt the butter in a roomy skillet. Add Parmesan cheese to the melted butter until a thick paste is formed. Add clams, parsley, garlic salt. Add the hot, drained spaghetti to the skillet and toss it with the creamy clam mixture until it's evenly mixed. Serve at once.

Swedish Fiskpudding

½ cup cooked rice, preferably cooked in milk
about 2 cups cooked fish
salt and pepper to taste
1 or 2 eggs
1 tablespoon melted butter

Butter a small stainless-steel bowl or a clean tin can which will fit into your pressure cooker. Canned, smoked, or leftover fish may be used. Combine all ingredients well and turn them into the mold. Place on the rack in the pressure cooker with one cup water and cook for eight minutes at full pressure. Let the pressure return to normal, then test the pudding by plunging a clean knife into it. If the knife comes out clean, the pudding is done. If not, place the lid back on the cooker and steam the pudding, without raising pressure, for another few minutes. Take care not to overcook this pudding or it will turn watery. Although it's usually served warm, fiskpudding is also good cold.

Variation: use mashed potato instead of rice.

Steamed Salmon Loaf

1 one-pound can salmon
2 eggs
8 soda crackers, crumbled
1 tablespoon lemon juice
salt and pepper to taste

Combine all ingredients and cook as for fiskpudding above. Canned cream of mushroom Soup for One, undiluted, makes a good sauce for this loaf. If you're using the canned soup, go easy on the salt in the recipe.

⟪ Kedgeree

Use your own smoked fish, smoked salmon from a can, or, as a last resort, well-drained canned salmon flavored with a drop of smoke seasoning.

2 cups, or about 14 ounces, smoked salmon or other fish
2 cups cooked rice
4 hard-boiled eggs, chopped
¼ cup melted butter
½ cup milk
salt and pepper as needed (but the salmon may be salty enough)

Toss all ingredients together in a heavy skillet over very low heat until warm. This serves four to six as a main dish and is especially good with chutney. Note: the rice should consist of dry, stand-apart grains and should not be overcooked.

Galley Tips: Canned Seafood
Make a quick one-dish meal by adding a can of tuna to a prepared, packaged macaroni-and-cheese dinner. Fold in a small can of peas, well drained. Heat through.

Make an economical tuna dip by mashing drained, canned white beans into a paste. Add tuna and mash well. Moisten with yogurt and season to taste.

Use canned tuna or salmon in your favorite chowder.

Creamed tuna over toast makes an excellent cruising meal because the toast adds crunch. Make it a one-dish meal by adding a drained green vegetable to the tuna mixture.

Assemble packaged scalloped potatoes according to the package directions. Add a can or two of tuna, a teaspoon of prepared mustard, and a topping of crushed potato chips.

Bake big Idaho potatoes in your stovetop oven, scoop out the skins, and mash the potatoes. Add milk to moisten and canned tuna plus some grated cheese if you have it. Pile this mixture back into the potato skins. Reheat in stovetop oven just before serving.

For a change, try making spaghetti sauce with canned fish, shrimp, or clams in place of meat.

Commercially canned mackerel, tuna, salmon or shrimp, or your own canned-aboard fish, make a delicious salad sandwich filling. When you have no celery, try grated cabbage, onion, or apple instead. Served on crackers, these salads make tangy canapes.

Make crisp tuna- or salmon burgers by mashing together the canned fish with half a cup or so (depending on how far you have to stretch the fish) of instant mashed potatoes, one or two eggs, and some finely minced onion. Form into burgers, dip in bread crumbs, and fry in hot fat until browned and crunchy. These burgers are hard to handle at first, but firm up as the eggs "set."

14. DESSERTS

Many considerations went into my collection of recipes for galley desserts. First, they can all be created without an oven, and you'll find stovetop baking instructions on page 15. I am also concerned with ease of stowage, so I have avoided traditional, sticky frostings except for the most special occasions. Ease of preparation and clean-up are also important in the small, water-short galley.

Even though cruising cooks can carry eggs for weeks, I have focused on recipes that use as few eggs as possible, and I have included some eggless cakes. Eggs are such a versatile food, and can be used in so many dishes where they are seen and tasted, that I dislike using them invisibly in baked goods unless they are important to the recipe.

Lastly, this chapter fulfills its promise to the sailor who has no refrigeration. Although this does rule out gelled and frozen desserts, some ingredients such as cream cheese, and some baked specialties such as soufflés and cream puffs, your crew will be so dazzled by these recipes, they'll probably never miss them. Here, and elsewhere throughout the book, consult the Glossary (page 229) if you encounter an ingredient which you think you cannot carry without refrigeration.

Fake Flan

After this recipe appeared in the first *Cooking on the Go*, it suddenly hit the headlines because *another* cookbook used the recipe, neglecting to tell readers that the can must be opened first. Heating an unopened can could result in an explosion, and the whole episode resulted in history's first cookbook recall. My original recipe remains safe and delectable today, but there is another new twist. I have also tried it with the homemade condensed milk recipe below. The result is a somewhat less creamy, more butterscotchy flan. Try them both. They're each delicious. Make servings small, possibly with fresh fruit as a sort of "chaser." The flan is extremely rich. Here's how to make it:

Take the label and top off a can of sweetened condensed milk and cover it tightly with foil. Place it on a rack in your pressure cooker with about an inch of water and cook at full pressure (15 pounds) for 30 minutes. Let it cool, then remove and slice the milk-turned-flan. Or, prepare one recipe sweetened condensed milk, pour it into a can, cover the top with foil, and cook it the same way. Cool the flan thoroughly before turning it out of the can.

Sweetened Condensed Milk

1 cup nonfat dry milk
⅔ cup sugar
3 tablespoons melted butter or margarine
⅓ cup boiling water

Although the original directions called for making this in a blender, I have also made it by mixing it with a balloon whisk. Work quickly and mix it very well to dissolve all the sugar and milk in this very small quantity of water. Use this as a substitute for one can of sweetened condensed milk in any recipe calling for that ingredient (viz., Key Lime Pie, Fake Flan, and Egg Nog).

Also, use this milk in coffee if you like light, sweet coffee, or make cocoa by adding sweetened condensed milk to boiling water in which you have dissolved a half teaspoon of unsweetened cocoa.

 ## Bread Pudding

This is a favorite with Carl and Jeanne Moesly aboard *Rigadoon*, who have sailed around the world twice. When using her oven, Jeanne bakes this in a bread loaf pan, but she has also baked it atop the stove in an eight-inch-square casserole dish.

4 slices toast
1 to 1½ cups dried fruit (raisins, fruit cake mix, etc.)
water or rum
2 eggs
2 cups milk
½ cup sugar
a pinch of salt
1 teaspoon vanilla
cinnamon sugar

Butter the toast on both sides and place two slices in the bottom of the pan. Cut it to fit the pan bottom if necessary. Soak the fruit in a small amount of water or rum to soften it, then drain and put it atop the toast. Top this with the other two pieces of toast after cutting them to fit in a single layer. Whisk together the eggs, milk, sugar, salt, and vanilla, and pour over the toast. Bake by the indirect Dutch oven method for 30 to 45 minutes, or until the custard tests done. Sprinkle with cinnamon sugar.

Stuffed Bananas

3 large or 6 small bananas
¼ cup dark rum
¼ cup raisins
¼ cup butter
½ cup confectioners' sugar
3 tablespoons finely chopped peanuts
12 candied cherries

You are making six servings so cut the bananas in half lengthwise and serve one whole banana per person. If bananas are large, cut lengthwise and then in halves and serve half a banana per person. If you're making this dessert ahead of time, dip the banana pieces in lemon juice to keep them white. Soak the raisins in the rum, the longer the better. Cream the butter and sugar together, then drain the raisins and add the rum to the butter cream. Beat until it's fluffy and all the sugar is dissolved. Using a grapefruit spoon, scoop a shallow trench in each banana piece and fill it with butter cream. Sprinkle with raisins and peanuts, and crown each serving with halved candied cherries.

Grilled Bananas

Slit one ripe banana per peson and drizzle a little honey inside. Force in a few chocolate chips, tiny marshmallows, or chocolate syrup. Grill the bananas over charcoal, slit side up, until the fillings have melted.

Flaming Bananas

Sauté one large, firm banana, or two small ones, per person in a roomy skillet with a generous layer of butter until the bananas have begun to soften but not wilt. Sprinkle with finely grated orange rind if you have some, about four tablespoons orange-flavored liqueur, and a tablespoon or two of sugar to create a glaze. At this point you can set the pan aside while you make and serve dinner. Just before serving, pour a quarter-cup of rum over the bananas, light it, and spoon the flaming syrup over the bananas until the fire is gone. Serve at once.

Cakes

⌦ Pitchpole Cake

Traditional upside-down cake can be baked in a skillet atop the stove or in an electric skillet, so you've probably used this technique at home on days when you didn't want to heat a large oven. You create the beauty of the finished cake by arranging fruit on the bottom of the pan. Let your imagination go to work with fruit, spots of jam, nuts, and maraschino cherries.

> 2 tablespoons butter or margarine
> fruit, nuts, coconut, etc.
> ⅓ cup butter or margarine
> ½ cup brown sugar
> 1 cup sugar (less if fruits are especially sweet)
> 1⅓ cups flour
> 2 teaspoons baking powder
> ½ teaspoon salt
> 1 teaspoon vanilla
> ⅔ cup milk
> 1 egg

Melt the two tablespoons butter in a heavy aluminum skillet for which you have a heavy, tight-fitting lid. Arrange well-drained fruit, fresh fruit, or what have you in the melted butter. Sprinkle it with the brown sugar. Then make a batter by creaming together the fat and sugar. Add the egg, then add the dry ingredients alternately with the milk. Finally, add the vanilla. Beat the batter smooth and pour it carefully over the arranged fruit. Bake, tightly lidded, over a medium flame with a flame shield for about 30 minutes or until the cake is spongy. Immediately turn it out onto a plate. Serve warm or cold, with tinned cream or fresh yogurt if you like.

Eggless White Cake

½ cup butter or shortening
1 cup sugar
2 cups flour (preferably cake flour)
½ teaspoon soda
½ teaspoon salt
1 teaspoon baking powder
1 cup sour milk or thinned yogurt
1 teaspoon vanilla

Cream the fat and sugar together, then add the dry ingredients alternately with the wet. Bake by the indirect Dutch oven method until the cake is springy to the touch and has started to pull away from the sides of the pan.

Note: packaged cake mixes can be baked without eggs, although they will be very tender and fine-crumbed, and will fall apart more easily. Eggless cakes made with a soda–sour milk base rather than with baking powder as a rising agent are firmer, and thus are easier to frost and to cut.

144

Can-ana Cupcakes

⅓ cup shortening or margarine
½ cup sugar
½ teaspoon cinnamon
¼ teaspoon ginger
1⅔ cups flour
1 egg
3 teaspoons baking powder
a pinch of salt
1½ cups mashed bananas
1 cup chocolate chips
½ cup chopped nuts (optional)

Cream the butter with sugar, spices, and egg, and blend in the dry ingredients alternately with the bananas. Fold in the chips and nuts. Clean some tall, thin cans such as those that soda comes in, and fill them no more than two-thirds full with batter. Arrange the cans on a rack in your pressure cooker (see pressure cooker indirect method, page 15) and bake about 30 minutes or until the cakes test done with a toothpick. Cool, remove the can bottoms, push out the cakes, and cut them each into two or three pieces to form cupcakes. Frost if desired, or sprinkle with confectioners' sugar.

Easy-Mix Gingerbread

1 egg
¼ cup sour milk or thin yogurt
¼ cup molasses
¼ cup honey
¼ cup salad oil
1 teaspoon baking soda
1 teaspoon ground ginger
1 cup flour

Pile everything into an eight-inch-square cake pan and work with a spoon until it's well blended. Pay special attention

145

to corners to make sure all dry ingredients are mixed in. Bake by indirect Dutch oven method about 25 minutes or until the cake is firm and springy. This is delicious alone or sauced with vanilla pudding or applesauce.

Sue's Cherry Cobbler

This recipe comes from Sue Moesly aboard *Svea*.

⅓ cup butter
1 cup flour
¼ cup sugar
½ teaspoon salt
½ teaspoon baking powder
⅓ cup nonfat dry milk powder
¾ cup water
½ teaspoon vanilla
1 can cherry pie filling

Melt the butter in a heavy skillet. Meanwhile, make a batter from the dry ingredients and water. Pour the batter over the melted butter, then add the fruit but do not stir. Cover the skillet and cook over a medium flame with a shield for about 30 minutes. The batter will rise around the fruit, form a cake on top, and brown around the edges. The cobbler is done when this topping is firm to the touch. To serve, spoon onto serving plates, cake-side down and cherries on top. For oven baking, bake at 350° for about 30 minutes.

🐚 Scrunch

> 1 can any flavor fruit pie filling
> 1 box one-layer yellow cake mix or ½ box two-layer cake mix
> ¼ to ½ cup butter

> Spread the pie filling in a square pan, sprinkle it with the cake mix, and dot it with chunks of butter or margarine. Bake by indirect Dutch oven method until the topping is lightly browned.

Fruit Cocktail Cake

This soupy batter can be mixed directly in the pan or in a sturdy plastic bag. The egg may be omitted.

> ½ cup white sugar
> ½ cup brown sugar
> 1 teaspoon baking soda
> 1 egg (optional)
> 1 teaspoon vanilla
> 1 one-pound can fruit cocktail, including juice
> 1 cup broken nuts
> 1 teaspoon salt
> 1 cup flour

Dump everything into a pan or bag and work it until it's well mixed. Bake by indirect Dutch oven method. This is a very moist, puddinglike cake.

⚓ Eggless Chocolate Cake

An easy-to-mix salad dressing (mayonnaise type) takes the place of both oil and eggs in this cake. There is no shortening to cream so you can mix it in the pan or in a plastic bag. An entire eight-ounce jar of salad dressing is used so there is no problem with leftovers.

> 2 cups flour
> 1 cup cold water
> ¾ cup sugar
> 4 heaping teaspoons unsweetened cocoa
> 2 teaspoons baking soda
> 1 cup (8-ounce jar) mayonnaise or salad dressing
> 2 teaspoons vanilla

Mix everything together in a bag or pan until well blended. Make sure no flour remains in corners. Bake about 30 minutes by indirect Dutch oven method. Cake is done when it is springy to the touch. The recipe fills an eight-inch-square pan.

Po'-Boy Chocolate Cake

Since this recipe appeared in the first *Cooking on the Go*, it has been baked in hundreds of galleys around the world. Even without eggs, the texture is firm and rich, and mixing is so easy!

> 1½ cups flour
> 1 teaspoon baking soda
> 3 tablespoons cocoa
> 1 teaspoon salt
> ½ cup sugar
> 1 tablespoon vinegar
> 5 tablespoons salad oil
> 1 cup cold water
> 1 teaspoon vanilla

Mix all the dry ingredients in an eight-inch-square cake pan. With the back of a spoon, make three holes in the mixture. Put the vanilla in one, the vinegar in the second, and the oil in the third. Pour the cold water over all. Work well with a spoon, paying special attention to the corners, and make sure no unmixed dry ingredients remain. Bake by the indirect Dutch oven method for about 30 minutes or until the cake is springy to the touch.

🐚 Crumb Cake

The topping bakes right on this moist, spicy cake, and mixing is easy because you use a pastry blender.

2 cups flour
1 teaspoon nutmeg
1 teaspoon cloves
½ teaspoon salt
2 teaspoons cinnamon
1 teaspoon baking soda
1 cup sugar
½ cup margarine or shortening
1 tablespoon molasses (optional)
¾ cup sour milk (sour any milk with a few drops of
  vinegar)
1 egg

Mix all the dry ingredients except for the baking soda in a roomy bowl. Cut in the shortening until the mixture is mealy. Save a half-cup of this mixture for the topping. Mix the egg, molasses, sour milk, and baking soda. Then quickly add it to the dry mixture and stir until the dough is evenly moistened. Pour it into a square cake pan, sprinkle with the reserved crumbs, and bake about 30 minutes by the indirect Dutch oven method.

🐟 Depression Cake

Many versions of this eggless cake have been given to me over the years. It originated in the 1920s when raisins were cheap and eggs and lard were costly. It is still of interest to the cruising sailor who wants to conserve eggs and shortening. Any cut-up dried fruit can be substituted for the raisins.

1 cup raisins
2 cups water
1 tablespoon butter, shortening, margarine, etc.
1 cup sugar
2 cups flour
2 teaspoons cinnamon
1 teaspoon nutmeg
1 teaspoon baking soda
pinch of salt

Cook the fruit and water together at a boil for at least five minutes. Drain the fruit, reserve the liquid, and add more water if necessary to make one and a half cups. Add the fat to the hot fruit, stirring to melt it. Mix the dry ingredients together and add to the fruit along with the liquid. Stir quickly but thoroughly until all the dry ingredients are well wetted. Bake in a square cake pan by the indirect Dutch oven method for about 35 minutes or until the cake is springy to the touch and the edges have begun to pull away from the sides of the pan. This cake is especially good with white frosting.

Apple Crumb Cake

½ cup raisins
2 cups graham cracker crumbs
2 cups applesauce
½ teaspoon cinnamon
¼ teaspoon vanilla
½ cup chopped nuts
⅓ cup brown sugar
¼ cup butter

Plump the raisins in boiling water for about ten minutes, and drain. Pour one cup of the crumbs into a cake or pie pan, cover with applesauce, and sprinkle with the vanilla, cinnamon, nuts, raisins, and brown sugar. Top with the remaining crumbs and dot with flecks of butter. Bake 25 to 30 minutes by the indirect Dutch oven method. Spoon into serving dishes and top with your favorite vanilla sauce or with thinned, instant vanilla pudding.

 Add-a-Can Cake

This moist, spicy cake is made without eggs and with an interesting choice of canned ingredients.

½ cup butter or margarine
1 cup brown sugar
1 can undiluted tomato soup or applesauce
1 teaspoon cinnamon
2 teaspoons baking soda
1 teaspoon nutmeg
2 cups flour
1 cup raisins
½ to 1 cup chopped nuts (optional)

Cream the butter with the sugar, then stir in the soup or applesauce alternately with the dry ingredients. Bake in a square pan by the indirect Dutch oven method 45 to 50 minutes or until the cake tests done.

Pies

⚓ Anti-Roll Pie Crust

This is so buttery, tender, and easy to make, I never use any other type of crust when baking a one-crust pie. Because it is made with butter or margarine, it browns readily in a stovetop oven. (Crusts made with shortening or oil take longer to brown.)

½ cup butter or margarine
1 cup flour, more if needed
1 tablespoon sugar (optional)

Melt the butter in a pie pan over low heat. Remove from heat and add the flour and sugar, mixing with a fork until the dough is well blended. If any oily pools remain, add more flour, one tablespoon at a time, until the dough has lost its greasy look. Portions vary, because flours and fats differ. With your fingers, press the crust around the sides and bottom of the pan, and flute the edges. Bake by the indirect Dutch oven method.

Coconut Pie Crust

3 tablespoons butter
1½ cups grated coconut
½ cup confectioners' sugar
1 tablespoon milk

Melt the butter in a pie tin over very low heat. Then take it off the heat, add the milk, then the sugar. Stir well and mix in the grated coconut. (Shredded coconut will make the pie too difficult to cut.) Press the mixture to the bottom and sides of the pan. Cool completely, then fill with your favorite pudding or pie filling.

Crumb Crust

1½ cups cookie and cracker crumbs
3 tablespoons butter
1 tablespoon sugar

When your cookies and crackers lose their snap in the damp sea air, give them a second life as pie crust. Just beware of using too high a proportion of salted crackers because of their salt content. Place the cookies and crackers in a brown paper bag or a canvas bag made for this purpose and roll or pound them until crumbed (see "Rum Dums," later in this chapter). Melt the butter over low heat, stir in the remaining ingredients with a fork until well blended, and press the mixture to bottom and sides of the pan. It's best if you bake this ten minutes in a stovetop oven, but the crust can also be used without baking.

🐚 Pie Fillings

Custard pie. Fill the uncooked crust with egg custard from your own recipe or a mix. Bake until the crust is browned and the custard set.

Fruit pies. My anti-roll crust does not adapt well to two-crust pies, but you can use a streusel topping. Make the crust, then fill it with a canned fruit pie filling. Top with a streusel made by rubbing a half-cup of flour and a quarter-cup brown sugar with a quarter-cup of butter. Bake until crust and topping brown.

Cream pie. Bake the pie shell until it's lightly browned, cool it, then fill with a cream filling or lemon filling.

Key lime pie. Ann Bolderson aboard *Nymph Errant* uses real key limes for this dessert, but you can also use Persian limes or bottled juice. Mix one to two cans sweetened condensed milk with the juice of six to twelve limes. With experience, you'll learn how much lime juice to use for just the tartness your family likes. Just a small amount of lemon or lime juice is enough to "set" the condensed milk, which turns to a custard in this recipe. Keep adding juice, blending with a whisk, and tasting. Start with one can of milk. Then if the pie shell is not filled enough, add a second layer. The filling firms up fast, so as soon as the desired taste is reached, spread the filling into the pie shell. Let it stand in a cool spot, but refrigeration is not necessary. This is so rich, we prefer the shallow, single-can version.

Cookies

Scotch Squares

¼ cup salad oil
1 cup brown sugar, firmly packed
1 egg
1 cup flour
¼ teaspoon salt
1 teaspoon vanilla
1 cup coarsely broken nuts

Blend the oil and sugar in a medium-size bowl, then add the egg and mix well. Stir in the flour, salt, and vanilla, then the nuts. Spread in an eight-inch-square pan and bake by the indirect Dutch oven method for about 30 minutes. Cut into squares, then cool.

Sandbars

1 cup butter
½ cup plus 2 tablespoons sugar
2½ cups flour

When made with real butter, this is a very rich and special dessert, but it can also be made with margarine. Cream the fat and sugar together until smooth, then work in the flour. The dough will be very stiff. Spread it in an eight-inch-square pan, taking care to make the dough an even depth throughout so it cooks evenly. Score shallowly with a sharp knife into 16 squares. Bake by the indirect Dutch oven method until they're lightly browned. Cut while warm, but let the bars cool before removing them from the pan.

🐚 Fry Cook Cookies

½ cup butter
1½ cups graham cracker or cookie crumbs
1 cup chopped nuts
about 3½ ounces flaked coconut
1 cup chocolate chips
1 can sweetened condensed milk (see page 140)

Melt the butter in a heavy skillet, at least ten inches in diameter, for which you have a tight-fitting lid. Add the remaining ingredients one by one, in layers. Then drizzle condensed milk over all. Cover the skillet tightly and bake over a low flame with a shield for 25 minutes or until the cookies are set. Cool, uncovered, 15 minutes. Then cut into wedges with a sharp knife and remove from the pan with a frosting spatula.

 Rum Dums

These cookies appear to be easy because they are not cooked, but you may have a problem making crumbs without a blender or food processor. I sewed a small bag out of heavy canvas. This is filled with stale bread or cookies and rolled and pounded to make crumbs. A sturdy brown paper bag may also be used. If you use a cloth bag, launder it often or it will attract bugs.

1 box (12 ounces) vanilla wafers
2 tablespoons cocoa
1 cup sifted confectioners' sugar, plus more for rolling cookies
1 cup chopped pecans
a few drops of imitation butter flavoring
3 tablespoons honey
¼ cup rum

Crush the cookies to make fine crumbs, then mix with the other ingredients. Work the mixture with your hands until it is thoroughly moistened. Form it into tight walnut-size balls and roll these in confectioners' sugar. Store in tightly lidded coffee cans or plastic containers.

🍪 Kettle Cookies

1½ cups rolled oats
⅓ cup chopped nuts
⅓ cup coconut
1 cup sugar
¼ cup butter
¼ cup plus 2 tablespoons milk
1 teaspoon vanilla

Mix the oats, nuts, and coconut by shaking them in a small bag. In a roomy saucepan, bring the sugar, butter, and milk to a boil and boil three minutes. Quickly add the vanilla, then the dry ingredients, and stir to mix thoroughly. Drop by teaspoonsful onto sheets of waxed paper and allow the cookies to dry several hours before storing.

Variation: An alternate recipe, which is prepared by the same method, calls for the following ingredients:

3 cups rolled oats
3 tablespoons cocoa
2 cups sugar
½ cup milk
1 teaspoon vanilla
¼ cup butter
½ cup peanut butter

Raisins or nuts can be added to this recipe (and raisins can substitute for coconut in the original recipe).

Cocoa Logs

¼ cup butter
1 cup chocolate chips
⅓ cup peanut butter
4 cups ready-to-eat, chocolate-flavored cereal

Melt the butter and chocolate chips in a heavy pan over very low heat. Add the peanut butter and stir until it's well blended. Add the cereal and mix well, then press quickly into a 9-by-13-inch pan. Cool, then cut into logs.

Coral Reefs

½ cup butter or margarine
32 marshmallows
1 teaspoon vanilla
5 cups Rice Crispies

Cook the butter and marshmallows over a very low flame until it's thick and syrupy. Remove it from the heat, and stir in the vanilla. Pour over the cereal in a big, buttered bowl and press into buttered pan(s). Let stand until cool, then cut into squares. These are best if made in dry, not humid, weather.

Steamed Desserts

Many types of sweets, from ordinary egg custard to traditional Christmas puddings, can be baked atop your galley stove by steaming. Old methods took hours, but a pressure cooker cuts those times in half. It's best not to use sea water for steaming because so much will evaporate that unpleasant residues will be left behind. Fresh water used for cooking need not go to waste; use it to rinse dishes.

Important: when making any steamed dessert, fill the mold

157

no more than two-thirds full to allow room for expansion during cooking. Before cooking, make a lid for the mold by covering securely with aluminum foil.

Although cooking can be done in custard cups to make individual servings, tin cans prove the most practical for the boatman. Simply rinse, dry, and save empty tins until you have enough for a batch of pudding, or use one large coffee tin for a single pudding. A stainless-steel bowl can also be used.

See the instruction book that came with your pressure cooker and other pressure-cooker cookbooks for more steamed dessert recipes.

Brown Betty

> 1 cup dry bread crumbs
> ¼ cup sugar
> ½ teaspoon cinnamon
> juice and rind of one lemon
> 3 medium apples, sliced, or 1 can pie-sliced apples
> ¼ cup butter, melted

Combine the dry ingredients, including the finely grated lemon rind, and alternate them in a buttered mold with layers of apples. Sprinkle with juice and butter. Cover the mold with foil and put it on a rack in the pressure cooker with a cup of water. Heat the cooker until steam is escaping forcefully. Place the regulator on the cooker and time the cooking 15 minutes after 15 pounds pressure has been reached. Cool the cooker, remove the betty, and serve it warm or cold with your favorite vanilla sauce.

Christmas Pudding

> 1 cup mixed candied fruit
> ¾ cup cut-up dates, raisins, currants, etc.
> ½ cup broken nuts
> 1 tablespoon flour

¼ cup shortening
4 tablespoons honey
1 egg
1½ tablespoons water or juice
½ cup flour (minus 1 tablespoon for coating)
¼ teaspoon salt
¼ teaspoon baking powder
¼ teaspoon cinnamon
¼ teaspoon nutmeg

Put the fruits and nuts in a paper bag with the tablespoon of flour and shake to coat. Cream the shortening with the honey, then add the egg and water. Add the dry ingredients, then the fruit-nut mixture, stirring well. Place in mold(s), filling no more than two-thirds full, and set on a rack in your pressure cooker with five cups water. Steam for ten minutes without the pressure regulator, then 20 minutes more at ten pounds pressure. Serve with your favorite vanilla sauce or with a hard sauce made by creaming two tablespoons butter with a half-cup of confectioners' sugar. Flavor with a tablespoon of brandy or rum.

⚓ Sunshine Pudding

1 tablespoon butter
1 tablespoon sugar
1 cup flour
2 teaspoons baking powder
½ cup sugar
¼ cup fine, dry bread crumbs
¼ cup butter
¼ cup orange juice (from powder)
¼ cup Grand Marnier
½ cup candied lemon peel, chopped

Use the tablespoon of butter to grease a one-pound coffee can or several smaller cans. Add the sugar and shake to coat the inside of the buttered can. Combine the dry ingredients. Cream the butter, sugar, and eggs, then add the dry ingredients alternately with the orange drink. Stir in the lemon peel and Grand Marnier. Put into the prepared tin(s), filling no more than two-thirds full. Cover with foil and steam ten minutes without the regulator, then 20 minutes more at ten pounds pressure. Cool the pudding in the can but remove the foil so the surface can dry somewhat.

Cherry Pudding

2 teaspoons butter
½ cup sugar
1 egg
½ cup sugar
1 cup flour
¼ teaspoon salt
3 teaspoons baking powder
1 cup milk
1 can pitted pie cherries, reserving juice and ½ cup cherries
½ cup flour (for dredging cherries)

Cream the butter with the sugar and egg, then add the dry ingredients alternately with the milk. Drain the cherries very well, save the juice, and coat the cherries with the half-cup flour. Fold them into the batter. Fill buttered mold(s) two-thirds full and place on a rack in the cooker with two cups water. Steam ten minutes without regulator, then 20 minutes at ten pounds pressure. Serve with:

Cherry Sauce

cherry juice (reserved from preceding recipe)
2 teaspoons cornstarch
¼ cup sugar
½ cup reserved cherries

Make a paste with the cornstarch and some of the liquid, gradually adding cherry juice and stirring to keep it from lumping. Heat over a low flame until it is thick, then remove from heat and gently fold in the cherries. Spoon the sauce over servings of cherry pudding.

Dessert Sauces and Toppings

 ## Chocolate Sauce

1 can sweetened condensed milk
1 or 2 packets pre-melted baking chocolate
½ teaspoon vanilla
a few drops of butter or rum flavoring

Mix thoroughly and serve over cake, cookies, custard, or pudding.

 ## Fruit Cream

⅔ cup (half a can) sweetened condensed milk
3 tablespoons lemon juice
1 small can fruit, cut up

Mix the lemon juice and condensed milk with a balloon whisk until thick. Fold in the fruit, then thin with juice from the canned fruit until the sauce is the desired thickness. Serve over cake, gingerbread, or plum pudding.

Tosca Topping

2 tablespoons butter
1 tablespoon flour
¼ cup chopped almonds
¼ cup sugar
2¼ tablespoons milk

Melt the butter in a small saucepan, add the remaining in-gredients, and bring to a boil. Spread over the warm cake and return the cake to your "oven" for a few minutes until the top-ping is glassy.

Other Toppings

Poke Cake. Bake or buy a plain cake, and poke it in an even pattern, but to varying depths, with an ice pick. Mix a half-cup of chocolate syrup with one or two tablespoons of rum, then pour this over the cake and let it soak in for several hours. Or, mix half a package of gelatin dessert with a half-cup of boiling water. Dissolve, then drizzle this over the poked cake. Let stand several hours.

Lemon Glaze. Mix three tablespoons of lemon juice with three tablespoons of sugar, stirring to dissolve. Spoon it over a warm cake.

Sugar Sprinkle. Confectioners' sugar can be sifted over a cake to flavor and decorate it. For a special effect, place a paper lace doily over the cake first, sift the sugar over it, then lift the doily. A lacy pattern will remain on the cake.

Cranberry Topping. Mash and warm a can of whole cran-berry sauce with a quarter-cup of rum. Spoon it over plain cake or pudding.

Mincemeat Sauce. Bring one-and-one-third cups ready-to-use mincemeat and a quarter-cup rum to a boil and remove from the heat. Serve over spice cake or gingerbread.

Marshmallow Frosting. Immediately after taking the cake from your stovetop oven, arrange rows of marshmallows on it.

Wait until the marshmallows begin to melt, then spread them. This topping does not hold up well overnight in damp weather so use it on cakes which will be finished in one day.

Cherry Topping. Combine one jar cherry preserves and two tablespoons Kirsch in a small saucepan and bring just to the boil. Delicious over vanilla pudding or custard pie.

Chocolate Glaze. Right after baking, sprinkle chocolate chips generously over the hot cake surface. Let stand a few minutes until the chocolate chips soften, then spread them like frosting. On cooling, this topping will form a hard glaze. This works best with real, not imitation, chocolate chips.

Coconut Crunch. Moisten grated coconut with honey, add some chopped nuts if desired, and spread over the top of a cooled cake. Broil in oven or with a propane torch until the coconut is delicately browned.

Galley Tips: Desserts

Any two-layer cake mix can be baked in your mini-oven and served as bar cookies. Mix with oil and eggs according to directions, but reduce the water to two tablespoons. To make brownies, add nuts to chocolate cake mix. To make raisin bars, add raisins to spice cake mix. Mix the batter then spread it in a square cake pan, bake until it's firm and springy, and cut into squares.

Vary instant pudding by adding peanut butter. First blend a quarter-cup creamy or chunky peanut butter with the milk, then add pudding mix.

Spoon instant pudding into ice cream cones instead of bowls.

Buy baby food puddings for a smooth, single-serve dessert treat in a throw-away container.

Shop for tinned cakes and cookies in supermarkets, gourmet shops, and health food stores.

In a corner of a locker, tuck away some birthday candles, icing in tubes with decorator tips, and other aids for festive occasions.

To make your skillet/Dutch oven into a tube pan, place a greased tin can in the center and fill it with raw rice, nuts and bolts, or other weight. Pour the batter around the tin.

Many dessert recipes call for completion with ice cream or whipped cream. When these are not available, substitute a dollop of yogurt, tinned cream, marshmallow cream, or instant vanilla pudding.

When baking bar cookies, add a bonus layer. Put half the batter in the pan, top with a layer of graham crackers, and add the remaining batter. Bake as usual.

For a change, make instant puddings with yogurt instead of milk.

It is not necessary to grease a pan to be used for baking cakes or bar cookies that will be served from the pan. Buy a small frosting spatula to make serving easier.

Since many of the cake recipes in this book are made without shortening and other hard-to-mix ingredients, they can be mixed in a throw-away plastic bag. Zip-Loc bags are one of the sturdier brands. Stand the bag up in a bowl, fill it with the ingredients, work and squeeze it until the batter is smooth, and strip the batter out into the pan.

15. CANAPÉS FROM CANS

This chapter calls for many unusual ingredients, so you might look through the recipes to make a special shopping and provisioning list for items you may not have aboard. You'll find canapé ingredients in all aisles of the supermarket, including areas where you may not normally shop. You'll find canned clam dip and smoked oysters with the canned seafood, pâté and caviar on the gourmet shelves, pickled eggs in the deli, cheeses that require no refrigeration in the dairy department. Cheeses in jars and squirt cans are usually stocked with the fancy crackers.

In addition to the recipes in this chapter, you'll find recipes for pickled vegetables which can be served as cocktail snacks in Chapter 19, and recipes for homemade snack breads and crackers in Chapter 12, and Chapter 21.

🐚 Hot Shrimp Dip

This recipe originated with Ann Glenn aboard the charter trimaran *Encore* in the U.S. Virgin Islands.

1 clove garlic
1 can shrimp soup, undiluted
½ pound grated cheese (Swiss if possible)
2 tablespoons sherry

Rub a small pan with the garlic, and discard the pulp. Put the cheese and soup into the pan and mix well. Heat over a low flame, then stir in the sherry just before serving with crackers, chips, or cubed French bread.

 ## Tuna Butter

> **1 can (7 ounces) tuna**
> **1 small sweet onion, minced**
> **½ cup butter or margarine**
> **½ teaspoon cinnamon**
> **a dash of dill weed**
> **a dash of lemon juice**

Drain the tuna well, then mash all the ingredients together until they're smooth and pasty. Spread this on crackers, or pack it into a small crock so guests can help themselves.

⚓ Beefed-Up Popcorn

> **½ cup popcorn, unpopped**
> **1 small jar (2½ ounces) dried chipped beef**
> **¼ cup butter or popcorn oil**

Pop the corn. Tear the beef into tiny pieces and cook it in butter or oil about three minutes. Pour it over the popped corn and toss to coat well.

 ## Popcorn Olé

> **½ cup popcorn, unpopped**
> **2 tablespoons Sloppy Joe mix from a packet**
> **¼ cup butter or popcorn oil**

Pop the corn. Stir the Sloppy Joe mix into the butter or oil in a small pan and heat over a low flame until the sauce is smooth.

Pour it over the popped corn and toss until it's evenly coated. Add salt if necessary.

Nutty Ham Spread

1 can deviled ham
an equal amount of peanut butter
2 tablespoons yogurt
½ teaspoon prepared mustard

Empty the can of deviled ham into a bowl, then fill the same can with any style peanut butter and add it to the ham. If you don't have mayonnaise or yogurt to moisten this, add a little chili sauce, ketchup, or pickle juice. Add the mustard, mix well, and serve on toast triangles or crackers.

Potted Cheese

This recipe from Jane Marriott aboard the charter yacht *Flying Fifty* in St. Thomas, Virgin Islands, is an ideal way to use scraps of drying cheese. It can be packed into one large crock, individual crocks, or large scallop shells.

1 pound sharp cheese
3 teaspoons finely minced onion
1 teaspoon dried parsley (3 teaspoons fresh if you have it)
1 teaspoon Dijon mustard
salt to taste
2 cloves garlic, mashed
a pinch of ground mace
2 tablespoons soft butter
2 to 4 tablespoons sherry
a dash of Tabasco sauce
a dash of Worcestershire sauce

Grate the cheese into a roomy bowl, add the other ingredients, and mix well. Pack the mixture into container(s) and keep in a cool place. It's best made ahead of time so flavors have time to blend.

🐚 Goolagongs

This is a tasty way to use boat-baked bread that is in danger of going moldy. Although store-bought bread can be used, it should be a firm-textured type. Trim the bread (save the crusts to make bread crumbs) and cut into even "fingers." Then dry these in the hot sun until they're crisp, which should take only an hour or so. Blend together equal amounts of peanut butter and salad oil, dip the pieces of bread, then roll each piece in bread crumbs that you have seasoned delicately with oregano and basil. If you don't eat them all at once, pack the leftovers in plastic or tin, tightly lidded.

Galley Tips: Canapes

Because it carries so compactly, unpopped popcorn is the most practical snack food to take on long voyages.

Make fritters using fruit, seafood, or vegetables, and drop them into hot fat by the half-teaspoon to make dainty cocktail snacks.

To make cocktail croutons and use up staling homemade bread, cut the bread into inch-size cubes and toss in a skillet with butter and McCormick's Salad Supreme seasoning until evenly coated.

Make a delicious barbecue by heating one can of luncheon meat, cubed, with a half-cup ketchup, one teaspoon mustard, and one tablespoon molasses. Serve with toothpicks.

String toothpicks with cubes of cheese, chunks of canned luncheon meat, pickled onions, olives, chunked pineapple, or what have you for color and variety.

Marinate halved artichoke hearts or mushroom caps, well drained, in vinegar and oil dressing for cocktail snacks.

Buy canned raw, unsalted nuts. (Salted nuts limit your menus and, being hygroscopic, may stale quickly once the can is opened.) Then you can prepare some a different way each day by tossing the nuts in a little hot oil in a skillet with garlic salt, cinnamon sugar, and other spices.

16. DRINKS

Hot Drinks for the Family

Butterscotch Punch

There are many ways to prepare nonfat dry milk to please those family members who simply can't get it down at room temperature. This hot drink is a delicious change from cocoa.

¾ cup brown sugar
½ cup water
1 tablespoon butter
1⅔ cups nonfat dry milk
5 cups water
a pinch of salt
1½ teaspoons vanilla

Using medium heat and a heavy saucepan, melt the sugar, stirring constantly, then add the half-cup water and bring to a boil. Add the butter and cook another minute or two. Reduce the heat and add the five cups water, dry milk, and other ingredients. Heat, stirring, until the milk is dissolved and the mixture is heated throughout, but do not boil. Serve with a dusting of nutmeg and a dollop of tinned cream if desired.

171

Russian Tea

> 1 small jar sweetened, orange-flavored breakfast drink mix
> an equal amount of sweetened instant tea mix
> 1 packet lemonade mix
> 2 cups sugar (optional)
> ½ teaspoon cloves
> ½ teaspoon cinnamon

To make Russian tea, place a teaspoon or so of the mixture into each mug and fill with boiling water. For those who prefer drinks that are not too sweet, this mix contains plenty of sugar in the prepared drink mixes without adding more. Others may prefer the entire two cups of sugar. I've deliberately avoided exact measures of tea, drink mix, and sugar because this mix is made to taste and so is the finished drink. Mix all dry ingredients and store in a tightly covered container. The mix is highly hygroscopic so don't double the recipe unless you can use large amounts in a short time. In damp sea air it will clump after a few weeks and acquire a bitter taste.

Hot Cocoa Mix

> 13 cups nonfat dry milk
> 1 pound sweetened chocolate drink mix
> 4 tablespoons confectioners' sugar
> 1 large (11-ounce) jar coffee creamer

Mix well and repackage in small jars or sealed plastic bags. To serve, place a quarter-cup of the mixture in a cup and fill with hot water. Stir. For extra richness, add a marshmallow to each serving.

172

Liqueurs

Basic Sugar Syrup

1 lemon peel, yellow only, blotted to remove excess oil
3 cups sugar
2 cups water

Boil sugar with water and lemon peel for five minutes, stirring often. Strain and cool. Store in a tightly lidded bottle or jar. This syrup is the basis for most homemade liqueurs. Since sugar does not dissolve readily in alcohol, this syrup should be used in any drink where sweetening is desired.

The following recipe originated with Sue Moesly aboard *Svea.*

Anise Liqueur

1⅓ cups vodka
1¼ cups basic sugar syrup
2 teaspoons vanilla
1 teaspoon anise extract
a few drops of yellow food coloring

Mix everything in a tightly lidded bottle or jar and let stand at least a week, turning from time to time, for flavor to ripen.

Crème de Menthe

1⅓ cups vodka
1¼ cups basic sugar syrup
1 teaspoon peppermint extract
2 teaspoons vanilla
a few drops of green food coloring

Prepare according to instructions for Anise Liqueur.

Coffee Liqueur

This homemade mimic of a famous coffee cordial is very popular with boatmen, and many versions of the recipe have been printed. This one from Ann Bolderson aboard *Nymph Errant* can be used right after mixing but, like all liqueurs, it improves with age.

> 3 cups sugar
> 4 cups water
> 12 rounded teaspoons instant coffee
> a fifth of vodka
> 3 teaspoons vanilla

Bring sugar, water, and coffee to a boil, simmer gently one hour, and cool. Stir in the vodka and vanilla. Bottle. Makes about two quarts.

Apricot Cordial

> 1 package (8 ounces or about 1⅔ cups) dried apricots
> 2 cups water
> ¾ cup sugar
> 2 cups vodka
> 1 cup brandy
> 1 teaspoon cinnamon

Cut up the apricots into a saucepan, add the water, and bring to a boil. Cover and reduce heat, then simmer 15 minutes. Put the sugar, vodka, brandy, and cinnamon in a roomy jar along with the cooked, cooled apricots, cover securely, and shake. Let it stand for about two weeks, turning the jar each day to help the flavors blend. Strain the liquid into another bottle, cork, and serve as a cordial or as a syrup over plain cake or pudding. The apricots can also be served over a plain dessert or as a relish with curry.

⚓ Citrus Liqueur

Peel the outer rind (no white) from two or three oranges, or three or four lemons or limes, and blot to remove excess oil. Combine this in a screw-top quart jar with one and a half cups superfine granulated sugar and three cups vodka or rum. Tightly lid the jar and store it in a cool, dark spot for two days. Strain to remove the rind, then pour the liquid back into the jar, lid, and let it stand in a cool, dark place to age for a week or two, shaking occasionally to help the sugar dissolve.

⟨⟩ Fruit Cordials

A variety of fruit-flavored syrups are sold in supermarkets, usually displayed with ice cream syrups in the pancake syrup department. To make a raspberry, blueberry, or other cordial, combine a half-cup fruit syrup with one and a half cups vodka and one and a quarter cups basic sugar syrup, two teaspoons vanilla, and a suitable food coloring if desired.

Cocktails

We have cruised for months at a time with no refrigeration, and find it no hardship to adjust to drinking iceless cocktails. Those which work best without ice are fruit drinks and, if you prefer dry flavors, rum or wine with soda or water. In all cases, make drinks weaker than you would if serving with ice, to compensate for the extra water that ice would add. With or without ice, these recipes work well.

🐚 Sangria

> 1 bottle dry red wine
> 1 lemon, sliced thin
> 2 tablespoons sugar
> ½ orange, sliced thin
> 2 ounces orange-flavored liqueur such as Grand Marnier
> 1 quart or liter club soda

Combine everything except the soda in a large pitcher, stir, and let stand about 20 minutes until the sugar dissolves. Add the soda and serve in tall glasses, portioning out the fruit slices. Add a maraschino cherry to each glass if you like.

🐚 Yellow Bird

Into each glass place a shot or jigger of rum as desired, and one tablespoon banana liqueur. Fill the glasses with canned orange-grapefruit juice.

🕊 Rum Squash

Squeeze half a lime, sour orange, or lemon into a glass and add sugar to taste. Add a jigger of rum and a twist of peel, then fill the glass with water.

176

Sampson Cay Smash

For those who like sweet drinks, this one is especially rich and unusual. It originated at Sampson Cay in the Bahamas.

4 cups mixed fruit juices, including 1 can apricot nectar
1 egg
¼ cup cream, fresh or canned
a dash of grenadine syrup
rum

If you'll be serving this drink with ice, reduce the juices to three cups. Combine all ingredients except the rum in a shaker and mix thoroughly. Put a jigger of regular rum, or pineapple or coconut rum, into each glass and fill with fruit juice mixture.

Special-Occasion Drinks

Hot Buttered Rum

This bracing hot drink is delicious, especially after a wet sail, or over the chessboard when you are fogged in. The spice mix can be made ahead of time and kept for a week or more. Although margarine has become an acceptable substitute for butter almost everywhere, this drink demands real butter.

1 cup butter
2 tablespoons sugar (more to taste)
½ teaspoon ground allspice
dark rum

Soften butter to room temperature and work in the sugar and allspice. Pack into a plastic tub and lid it tightly. To serve, place a teaspoon of the butter mixture into a mug, add a shot of rum, and fill the mug with boiling water.

🦉 Glögg

This hot, pungent drink is served at Swedish celebrations, particularly at Christmas and Lucia Day. It can be made ahead of time, then heated just before serving.

1 cup sugar
1 cup raisins
¼ teaspoon cardamom seed
5 cloves
1 cup vodka
a small piece of ginger
¼ cup sweet red wine such as port
a fifth of dry red wine
¼ cup blanched whole almonds

Combine everything but the wines and almonds in a heavy stainless-steel or enameled pan. (Wine will stain aluminum.) Heat but do not boil. Add the wine and heat, without boiling, for 30 minutes. Add the almonds and serve in small cups with spoons for eating the almonds and raisins.

⚓ Egg Nog

Sweetened, condensed milk is your shortcut to making this holiday favorite. (For directions on how to make your own condensed milk, see page 140.)

6 eggs
1 teaspoon vanilla
2 cans sweetened condensed milk
grated rind of 1 lemon or lime
a dash of bitters
2 cups rum

Combine all the ingredients in a roomy bowl and beat with a balloon whisk or egg beater until well blended. If desired, sprinkle each serving with a whisper of nutmeg.

Part III

SPECIAL SITUATIONS

17. BOAT CAMPING

When you camp, you sleep in a tent and cook outdoors. When you yacht, you have a boat which has complete living facilities including a built-in galley. Then there is an outdoor life halfway between the two. It is boat camping, when you sleep on the boat but must cook in the cockpit or on the beach. Many small boats have cuddy cabins with vee berths and perhaps a head. On others, you can sleep on convertible seats under a dodger or tent. Eating, cooking, and washing dishes are accomplished with portable, camp-style equipment. My husband and I have lived for as long as three weeks at a time in this sort of lash-up, cooking on our knees in the cockpit when we were anchored, and cooking ashore when we docked or pulled up on the beach.

Here are some tips for yacht living on a runabout budget:

- Invest in a weathertight dodger or tent for the entire boat. You need added area for dressing, cooking, and privacy. Without the dodger you're stuck in the cuddy on rainy days, eating raisins.

- Don't construct a built-in galley. Keep your cooking setup portable so you can cook on the beach or at anchor. Often in boat-camping you'll be able to find campgrounds where there are grills, tables, faucets, and other luxuries.

- Collapsible plastic water jugs with built-in spigots are easy to carry and stow and they give you running water anywhere.

- The more ice chests you have room for, the better. Rigid types double as seats and work surfaces. Foldaway, fabric types serve as extras for times when you have lots of food and ice, and when you want to tote home a load of fresh fish. Keep one ice chest for drinks, another for food, if possible.

- Buy at least a one-burner portable campstove and make a folding wind screen for it. Three pieces of sheet aluminum, linked together so they will fold flat, do the job.

- Carry utensils in a "roll" made out of sturdy fabric. Stitch in pockets for knives, the spatula, pancake turner, and other needs. Tied into a compact roll, this easily goes ashore with you. If possible, add grommets or ties so it can be hung in a tree or rigging. Keep utensils at a basic minimum but include a double-geared can opener and at least one sharp knife.

- Include a length of clothesline to string up around the boat or campsite to hang gear and to dry towels.

- Paper plates are bulky and costly, and they present a disposal problem. If you do plan to use them for some meals, take wicker or plastic holders for them. It's no fun to eat perched on a helm chair with a floppy paper plate leaking potato salad through to your jeans.

- If you will be traveling for very long periods in a very small boat, living backpacker-style, a good reference book is Fred Powledge's *The Budget Backpacker's Food Book* (David McKay Company). For bigger boats, see Phyllis Bultmann's *Two Burners and an Ice Chest* (Prentice-Hall, Inc.)

Here are a few of my favorite boat camping recipes. Let them serve as the start of your own boat camping recipe collection based on family tastes and the equipment you have room to carry.

Shrimp Boats

2 pineapples
1 can (6½ to 7 ounces) shrimp
2 small cans white chunk chicken
½ cup diced radishes
3 green onions, sliced
1 small zucchini, diced
1 cup vanilla yogurt
½ cup rum

Halve the pineapples, leaving the green on for looks. Hack the fruit out of the shells, save about a cup of it to put into the filling, and put the rest on ice for a different use later. In a sturdy plastic bag, toss together all the ingredients except the yogurt and rum. This step can be done at home, if you like, and the filling kept on ice for a day or two. Portion the filling into the pineapple shells, sprinkle with rum, and then spoon the yogurt on top. Makes four shrimp boats.

Spam Bombs

This unusual combination of ingredients produces a very popular dish.

1 can Spam
1 one-pound can sauerkraut
1 can apple pie filling

Tear off four generous squares of heavy-duty aluminum foil. Cut the Spam into four slices and place them on the foil. Top with the well-drained kraut, then the pie filling. Bring up the sides of the foil and twist tightly to form well-sealed packages. Place them on the grill, Spam-side (bottom) down, and grill until the Spam is browned and the bomb heated through. Eat right from the foil.

🍃 Greek Lamb Stew

This elegant recipe is made at home, packaged in sealed, boilable bags, and is kept on ice or frozen to be reheated on your camp stove. Sealable, boilable bags are salvation for the boat camper as well as for the racing cook. This recipe serves eight, so for a smaller crew take only as much as you need. If you expect to serve this stew over rice, that too can be cooked ahead of time and sealed separately in a boilable bag.

> 3 pounds lean stewing lamb, cubed
> 1 large onion, diced
> ¾ cup dry white wine
> 2 cups water
> 2 tablespoons salt and a dash of pepper
> 1 tablespoon dill weed
> 1 bay leaf
> 2 packages frozen artichokes or 1 large can artichokes
> 2 tablespoons flour
> juice of one large lemon (¼ cup)
> 3 eggs

Brown the lamb in a large, heavy pot, a few pieces at a time. Add the onion. When the meat is all browned, return it to the pot and add a half-cup of the wine. Cover and simmer 15 minutes. Add the water and seasonings, and cook until the meat is tender. Remove the bay leaf and add the artichokes. If the artichokes were frozen, cook until they're tender. Drain the juice from the stew and package the meat mixture, saving the juice. Add water to the juice to make three cups. Blend the flour gradually into the remaining quarter-cup of wine to make a paste, then bring the three cups liquid to a boil and add the flour paste. Cook, stirring constantly, until it's smooth and thickened. Beat the eggs and lemon juice until the mixture is very light and fluffy, then add the boiling gravy. Cool, then package this separately.

To assemble this meal, put an inch or two of water (which can be used later) in a roomy pot and bring it to a boil. Add the meat, sauce, and rice pouches and heat thoroughly. Place some hot rice on each plate, top with lamb, then cover with the egg sauce.

See the instruction book that came with your bag-sealing appliance for additional tips about carrying foods this way.

Packet Boat

The real secret to this one-dish meal is the wrap because it must be completely sealed and sturdy enough to take turning without tearing. Although regular foil can be used, heavy-duty foil is extra insurance. Let each family member make one so there will be no squabbles about unwanted vegetables. For *each* packet:

> **1 hamburger, hot dog, sausage, lamb patty, or pork chop**
> **1 potato, scrubbed and sliced**
> **1 carrot, peeled and sliced**
> **½ onion, sliced**
> **green or yellow canned vegetable (optional)**
> **2 tablespoons catsup**
> **salt and pepper**

Place the meat on a large square of foil and add the other ingredients. Bring up the two opposite sides of the foil, press together, and roll down to meet the food but not too tightly. Steam will expand the package. Now fold the sides twice towards the middle of the package. Place it over the grill with well-started coals and turn it every 15 minutes or so—more often if the fire is too hot or the grill too close to the coals. Test one packet after 30 minutes. Take care opening these because there will be steam and scalding juices. Ideally, the packets should slow-cook for about 45 minutes.

18. THE MOVEABLE FEAST

Not everyone who eats aboard a boat cooks on the boat. This chapter is written for the roving host who prefers to do all the cooking at home, using the galley only to make coffee or perhaps to heat casseroles brought from home. Galley cooks who have microwave ovens aboard find them perfect for quick warm-ups. Other cooks plan other ways to keep hot foods hot and cold foods cold so meals can be presented without so much as a glance at the galley.

These recipes were chosen because they leave home complete and ready to serve. Stackable, leakproof plastic containers (Tupperware, Superseal) can be filled with salads, cold meats, and cold vegetable courses, garnished to perfection, and then stacked in an ice chest. Wide-mouth thermal containers can be used to carry soups if you want a hot first course. The gallon-size Igloo container is ideal for toting thick stews, baked beans, boiled potatoes, or steamy franks.

It's important, for food safety, that cold dishes be kept below 45° and hot dishes do not get cooler than 140°. Accomplish this by chilling cold foods thoroughly at home and keeping them in well-filled ice chests. Hot foods, too, can be carried in ice chests without the ice, in insulated containers, or wrapped in many layers of newspaper.

You can put together entire and complete tote-to-the-boat meals from the following recipes:

Fish-and-Potato Salad

4 medium potatoes, cooked
1 cup thinly sliced celery
¼ cup minced green pepper
2 tablespoons minced kosher dill pickle
1 cup sour cream
1 tablespoon prepared mustard
2 scallions, minced
½ teaspoon paprika
about 2 cups cooked fish
2 fresh tomatoes
hard-boiled eggs
dill weed

Slice the cooked potatoes thinly and layer them on the bottom of a plastic container. Sprinkle them with the celery, green pepper, and pickle. Mix together the sour cream, mustard, paprika, and minced onion. Flake the fish and check it well for bones, then sprinkle it over the potato mixture. Top it all with the sour cream dressing. Garnish with wedges of tomato and hard-boiled egg, and sprinkle with dill weed. Cover and chill, then keep it cold until served. Makes four main dish servings.

Vegetables and Brown Rice

1½ cups raw brown rice, cooked and cooled
¾ cup shredded carrot
¾ cup shredded zucchini
2 scallions, minced
¼ cup chopped parsley
2 tablespoons vinegar
2 tablespoons oil
salt and pepper to taste

Toss everything together in a large bowl, then transfer it to a lidded plastic container which has been lined with leaf lettuce.

188

Garnish with carrot curls and sprigs of parsley, and keep it cold until serving time. This is best made the day before, to allow thorough chilling and blending of flavors. It serves four as a main dish and eight to ten as a side dish.

⚓ Beef Belay

2 cups sour cream
½ cup red wine
1 clove garlic, minced
salt and pepper
½ teaspoon basil
3 cups cooked beef, diced
½ cup ripe olives
½ cup shredded carrots
½ cup minced fresh parsley
cherry tomatoes

Whisk the sour cream, wine, garlic, and herbs to make a smooth dressing. Toss the beef, olives, carrots, and parsley together, then toss with the dressing. Pile into a carry-serve container and garnish with cherry tomatoes.

Chicken en Gelée

1 whole chicken breast per person
lemon juice, thyme, parsley, tarragon, salt, pepper

For each four to six servings:

1 cup water
1 cup dry white wine
1 package unflavored gelatin
1 teaspoon granular chicken bouillon

Pull the skin off the chicken and remove the bone. Sprinkle the breasts with lemon juice, arrange them flat, and sprinkle them with herbs. Roll and tie them. Brown well on all sides in a

189

little hot butter, then add the bouillon, water, and wine and simmer until the chicken is tender, or about 15 minutes. Arrange the chicken in a plastic container from which it will be served. A plastic cold-cut keeper is ideal. Soften the gelatin in one cup cold water, then add it to the hot liquid in the pan. When the gelatin has dissolved completely, pour the liquid into a bowl and refrigerate until it just begins to set. Cut the strings off the chicken and spoon the gelatin mixture evenly over the breasts in their container. Press in garnishes such as rings of hard-cooked egg or colorful bits of raw vegetables, so they will set in the gel. After the gelatin hardens, add more garnishes such as radish roses. Cover the container and chill thoroughly. Keep cold until serving time. This is best served at the table.

🐚 Beef in Horseradish Sauce

>   2 pounds flank steak or top round
>   meat tenderizer
>   salt and pepper
>   2 one-pound cans whole beets

Sprinkle the steak with the tenderizer according to manufacturer directions, season, and broil to desired doneness. Cut it slantwise into thin slices and arrange them in a plastic container or platter. A 9-by-13-inch cold-cut keeper is a good carrier-server. Arrange the well-drained beets around the meat. Wrap or cover, and chill. Just before serving (this is served cold), pour on the following sauce:

>   2 green onions, minced
>   ¼ cup prepared horseradish
>   1 cup sour cream
>   a pinch of sugar
>   a sprinkle of dill weed

Whisk all ingredients together and carry cold in a well-lidded container.

Veal in Caviar

Baste a boneless veal roast with bacon, garlic, salt, thyme, and vermouth as you roast it until it tests done (internal temperature 150°). Cool, slice, and arrange for serving. Chop the bacon, mix it with the pan juices, and spoon it lightly over the slices. Chill and carry cold. Just before serving the cold meat, sauce with:

1½ cups sour cream
2 teaspoons Dijon mustard
1 tablespoon lemon juice
2 tablespoons red or black caviar

Whisk all these ingredients together and carry them separately in a well-lidded container, kept on ice. Serve this dish at the galley table; it calls for knives and forks.

Potato Salad One-Dish

6 medium potatoes, peeled, diced, and cooked tender
2 scallions, minced
1 cup creamy onion or cucumber flavor salad dressing
2 stalks celery, diced
1 can (12 ounces) corned beef or 1 package (16 ounces) knockwurst

Cook and drain the potatoes and, while they're still hot, toss them with the scallions and salad dressing. If you're using corned beef, chill it and cut it into cubes. If you use knockwurst, cut it into thin slices. After the potato mixture cools, fold in the remaining ingredients, adjust the seasonings, and pile the salad into a carry-serve container which has been lined with leaf lettuce if you like. Garnish, lid, chill, and keep on ice until serving time. A main dish for four or five.

191

Tuna Salad One-Dish

6 medium potatoes, peeled, diced, and cooked until tender
1 cup mayonnaise
1 package (10 ounces) frozen peas or mixed vegetables
2 large (12-ounce) cans tuna, drained
1 teaspoon salt (or to taste)
pepper as desired
½ cup yogurt
tomatoes and parsley for garnish as desired

Drain the potatoes after cooking and, while they are still warm, mix in the mayonnaise. Cook and drain the frozen vegetables. Cool the potatoes and vegetables, then gently fold in the remaining ingredients. Pile into a carry-serve container which has been lined with leaf lettuce if you like, garnish for serving, and chill. Keep on ice. This serves eight to ten as a main dish.

Ratatouille in Pepper Shells

8 small green peppers, halved and seeded
1 green pepper, diced
1 medium onion, diced
1 clove garlic, mashed
2 tablespoons olive oil
2 small zucchini, diced
1 eight-ounce can tomatoes, partly drained
salt and pepper to taste

Set aside the 16 pepper halves. Stir-fry the onion and garlic in hot oil, gradually adding the diced pepper and zucchini. Add the tomatoes and cook until all the vegetables are just crisp-tender. While this cools, cover the pepper halves with boiling water for five minutes, drain, and plunge them into ice water. They should be crisp-tender. Drain them well, arrange in a carry-serve container, fill with the other vegetables, and keep cold until serving time.

192

🐚 Stuffed Tomatoes

Find a container which will comfortably carry the number of tomatoes you want to serve (one tomato per person). Cut each tomato into wedges, cutting not quite through to the bottom so the tomato fans out slightly. Place each tomato on a lettuce cup in the container. Grate enough cheese (about an ounce per tomato) for filling. Moisten with mayonnaise. Spoon the filling into each tomato and top with crumbled, cooked bacon. Lid and chill. Provide two serving spoons for removing to plates.

🦅 Vegetable Kabobs

Choose small skewers which will fit into one of your carry-serve containers. String them with a variety of cherry tomatoes, mushroom caps, and parboiled chunks of carrot, zucchini, cauliflower, or other vegetables. Arrange them in the container, then drizzle with Italian dressing and marinate until served. Take pincher-type tongs for serving. Plan one kabob per person. Chill, carry in ice chest, and serve cold.

🐚 Lemon Fluff

graham cracker crumb crust
3 egg whites
¼ teaspoon cream of tartar
⅓ cup lemon or lime juice
1 can sweetened condensed milk

Press the crumb crust into an eight-inch-square plastic container. Add the cream of tartar to the egg whites and beat them stiff. Mix the juice into the condensed milk, then quickly fold in the egg whites until the mixture is blended. Spread it into the crust, cover with a sprinkling of graham cracker crumbs if you like, lid the container, and chill. An aerosol container of whipped cream carried in the same ice chest will make a pretty garnish for this dessert. At serving time, cut the fluff into nine squares and serve with a pancake turner.

🐚 Individual Cheesecakes

24 vanilla wafers
16 ounces cream cheese
¾ cup sugar
2 eggs
1 tablespoon lemon juice
1 teaspoon vanilla
1 can cherry or blueberry pie filling

Place 24 cupcake papers in cupcake pans and put a vanilla wafer in each one. Using an electric mixer, blend the other ingredients except for the pie filling until smooth. Divide this among the 24 cupcake papers and bake 15 to 20 minutes at 375°. The filling will be firm. Cool thoroughly, then top each cake with a tablespoon of pie filling, arrange in carrying container(s), and chill until served. If these cakes are to be eaten from the hand, use two cupcake papers each and, if your crew are cheesecake lovers, plan two cakes per person.

🐚 Crumbkin Pie

1 crumb crust (see page 152)
1 envelope unflavored gelatin
¼ cup rum
4 eggs
⅔ cup sugar
1 cup canned pumpkin
½ teaspoon ginger
½ teaspoon cinnamon
¼ teaspoon mace
¼ teaspoon cloves
1 cup cream, whipped

Press the crust firmly into the bottom of an eight-inch-square carry-serve container. Soften the gelatin in the rum, then stand the container in simmering water and shake it gently until the gelatin dissolves. Beat the eggs, gradually adding the sugar until the mixture is light and smooth. Stir in the pumpkin and spices, then the gelatin. Fold in the whipped cream and pile the mixture lightly into the crust. Garnish with a few more crumbs if you like. Chill. To serve, cut into nine squares and lift out with a small pancake turner.

Here are some general suggestions for keeping your carry-aboard meal as carefree as possible. The object is to do everything at home.

- Don't plan a roast or loaf that will require carving at the last minute. Slice your roasts at home, arrange in a shallow container, and garnish.
- Slice and butter breads, arrange them for serving, and cover tightly with foil or plastic wrap.
- If you're taking a soup course, choose a smooth soup that can be sipped from mugs, to eliminate spoons and bowls.
- Don't plan on unmolding gelatin salads at the last minute. Make mousses and other molded dishes in plastic containers, and garnish them at home. To serve, cut them into squares and serve with a pancake turner.
- If guests will be eating from their laps, don't serve meats that will require knife-and-fork attention. Some of the recipes here are best suited for serving at the galley table, with real dishes and cutlery. Others can be served on plastic plates with plastic utensils.

19. PRECOOKING AT HOME

The last chapter dealt with complete dishes which can be cooked at home, to be carried along and presented without cooking. The recipes here, although they, too, are made where you have supermarkets and full kitchen equipment, are meant to be eaten days, weeks, and—in the case of the fruitcake— even years later.

It is part of the fun of planning a voyage or extended cruise to cook and preserve foods. It saves money, and it also provides a warm link with home when you can have, miles from port, preserves made from blueberries you picked yourself, a pie made from apples you picked and dried yourself, or a casserole made with the chicken you bought on sale and canned without salt or preservatives.

Canning meat is a simple matter of putting it raw into sterilized jars and processing it according to time charts, which vary according to the type of pressure cooker or canner you are using.

If you have never canned before, get a basic canning how-to book which will tell you about techniques and equipment as well as how to can everything from pickles to pork roast. Even if you have a lot of canning experience, I'd suggest that you write to the manufacturer of your pressure cooker for canning directions because cooking times and pressures have changed in recent years.

I begin a cruise with a good supply of home-canned meats in glass jars, plus a supply of extra canning lids. The reusable canning jars are saved and, when fresh meat is available or when the fishing is good, I replenish our canned goods locker. All my canning is done in the same four-quart Presto pressure cooker I use for cooking and baking aboard. Canning times are longer if you use a pressure cooker rather than one of the large canners, so follow manufacturer directions precisely.

The canning recipes given here assume that you know the basics of canning. If you don't, there are many books available. I especially like *The Complete Book of Home Preserving* by Ann Seranne, *Putting Food By* from the Stephen Greene Press in Brattleboro, Vermont, and the cheap but helpful booklets available from the U.S. Department of Agriculture, Office of Communication, Washington DC 20250. Your county home extension home economist can also provide more specific instructions for preserving unusual foods, such as moose or fiddleheads, which are common to your home area.

Commercially canned fruits and vegetables are cheaper than those you can yourself (unless you grow them yourself, too) so concentrate instead on canning things you can't buy: meat, unusual combinations, old family preserves recipes, and types of pickles and relishes which aren't available commercially.

⟨𝓂⟩ Caponata

3 medium green peppers, chopped
3 medium onions, chopped
½ cup olive oil
4 large stalks celery
2 medium eggplants
2 large (28-ounce) cans tomatoes
1 one-pound can pitted black olives
2 tablespoons capers
5 teaspoons vinegar
2 tablespoons sugar
2 cloves garlic, well mashed

Using a roomy kettle, sauté the peppers and onions in about half the oil. Add the celery, then the eggplant, continuing to stir and sauté, adding remaining oil as needed. Stir in the remaining ingredients and cook, uncovered, for about 15 minutes. Pack into five one-pint jars which have been well washed and scalded and which are still hot. Seal with sterilized two-part lids and process in a pressure canner at ten pounds pressure for 25 minutes. Serve as a relish or on crackers as an appetizer.

⚓ Pepper Relish

12 green and 12 red bell peppers
12 medium onions
2 cups vinegar
3 teaspoons pickling salt

This is an easy recipe if you have a food processor. Chop the peppers and onions, cover them with boiling water, and let stand about five minutes. Drain well, add the remaining ingredients, and boil ten minutes. Pack hot into scalded jars and seal with scalded lids.

My Own "Groenola"

There are probably as many granola recipes as there are boats, all of them involving raw oats and other seeds or grains, baked and toasted with oil and honey. Although I've tried many of the recipes and found them good, this one is my favorite. Cost and calories are outrageous, but this nourishment-packed food can be served for breakfast or eaten dry any time as a snack.

> 5 cups rolled oats
> 1 cup whole, natural almonds
> 1 cup sunflower seeds
> 1 cup sesame seeds
> 1 cup shredded coconut
> 1 cup wheat germ
> ½ cup nonfat dry milk
> 1 cup vegetable oil
> 1 cup honey
> 1 teaspoon salt
> ½ to 1 cup raisins
> ½ to 1 cup cut-up dried apricots

Combine all dry ingredients except dried fruits in a large bowl and mix well. Mix together the oil and honey and pour over the dry mixture, tossing to coat well. Spread in a large rectangular baking pan and bake at 350°, stirring every ten minutes, for about 45 minutes or until the oats are lightly browned. Cool before adding raisins and apricots. Although some recipes call for adding dried fruits during all or part of the baking, I find this makes them too tough. Store in tightly lidded jars, cans, or sealed plastic bags. Serve for breakfast, with milk. To use as a snack food, form the mixture tightly into small balls while it's still warm from the oven, let them cool thoroughly, and store them in airtight containers.

Jamola

½ cup butter or margarine
⅓ cup sugar
⅓ cup jam
2 cups uncooked oatmeal
1 cup whole natural almonds
1 cup raisins or diced dates

Combine the butter and sugar with the jam and cook in a large saucepan until smooth. Remove from heat and stir in the oats and almonds until they are well blended. Spread the mixture evenly in a 9-by-13-inch cake pan and bake at 325° until it's lightly browned, stirring occasionally. Remove from oven, add the raisins or dates, and stir several times as it cools. Package lightly. Eat it dry as a snack, or serve with milk.

Homemade Grapenuts

3½ cups whole-wheat flour
1 cup brown sugar
1 teaspoon salt
2 cups sour milk
1 teaspoon soda

Mix the dry ingredients, add the sour milk, and stir to moisten. Spread the mixture a quarter-inch thick in a pan or pans and bake at 375° for 15 minutes. Cool, then put it through a grain mill or food grinder. When it's thoroughly dry, store it in tightly lidded jars.

Anniversary Fruitcake

A properly baked and wrapped fruitcake will last, not just weeks into your voyage, but for years. In olden times, when this type of cake was popularly served as a wedding cake, pieces were saved to be brought out on special anniversaries—including the tenth and even the twenty-fifth! Save pieces of linen from old tablecloths, frayed dinner napkins, or worn kitchen towels. Wash and iron them carefully, then wrap each fruitcake in linen and soak it in wine or brandy. Then wrap heavily in foil or, for long-term keeping, bury the linen-wrapped and brandy-soaked cake in a tin surrounded by sugar. Although keeping qualities of fruitcakes are excellent, they should be stowed in the coolest part of the boat—not under a hot deck or near the engine room. Although many fruitcake recipes call for mixed candied fruit or for citron, many people don't like the bitter taste of citron (which is also contained in the mixed fruit), so it's best to avoid it. Some family traditions demand a light-colored cake. Others prefer the darker version. In both cakes, the object is to cram a maximum of fruit into a minimum of dough.

¾ **cup shortening**
1½ **to 2 cups sugar**
5 **eggs**
1 **teaspoon vanilla**
4 **cups flour**
1 **teaspoon baking powder**
1 **teaspoon salt**
1 **pound** *each* **candied cherries, candied pineapple, chopped walnuts, and raisins**

Cream the butter and sugar, add the eggs, and beat until creamy. Beat in the vanilla, then add the dry ingredients which have been sifted together. When the batter is smooth, fold in the fruits and nuts evenly. This recipe will fill two loaf pans or five medium tin cans, filling two-thirds full to allow for rising. Bake an hour at 350° for loaves, a shorter time for pans. Test with a toothpick.

After baking, cool the cakes partially in their pans, then remove, cool, and wrap them for storage. To serve, cut them with a serrated knife. These cakes are not recommended for same-day eating. They'll be easier to cut on the second day, and will taste better as they age.

Note: other types of fruit, such as chopped dates or currants may be substituted. So can other nuts, such as pecans. The batter in this cake will be light. If your family prefers a darker, spicier fruitcake, add two teaspoons cinnamon, one teaspoon of nutmeg, and a quarter-teaspoon of cloves to the dry ingredients.

Potato Lefsen

This classic restorable bread is still popular with Scandinavian-American families. Traditionally, lefsen are stored in round, wooden boxes. Store them in your boat so they are protected from moisture and from breakage.

½ cup mashed potato
1½ cups water
1½ cups milk
2 tablespoons butter
½ teaspoon baking powder
a pinch of salt
2 to 2¼ cups flour

If you have no leftover mashed potatoes, make instant mashed potatoes. Bring the water to a boil, remove from heat, and add the milk. Stir in the potatoes, butter, and baking powder and beat for one minute. Add the flour and mix well. Knead this to a firm mass, adding flour if necessary. Pinch off balls of dough and roll each to a thin circle. Bake on a hot, ungreased griddle. (Pioneers used the entire surface of a hot cookstove.) Brown the lefsen on one side, then turn and brown the other side. Cool on racks until they are thoroughly dry. Store. To serve, sprinkle the lefsen with water and stack them between dish towels until they become pliable. Fold them around butter, with jam if you like.

Rusk

You can buy commercially made rusk, which is usually sold for teething babies, but your own will be delicious.

1 teaspoon baking soda
1½ cups whole-wheat flour
1½ cups unbleached white flour
1 heaping teaspoon baking powder
½ teaspoon salt
1 cup sour cream
1 cup sugar

Mix the dry ingredients, except for the sugar. Stir the sugar into the sour cream. Then combine the wet and dry ingredients to make a thick batter. Spread it into a greased and floured 9-by-13-inch baking pan and bake at 350° until it is springy to the touch and begins to pull away from the sides of the pan. Let the rusk cool and then cut it into squares. Split each square, arrange them on cookie sheets, and bake again at 350° until they are golden. Let them cool and dry thoroughly, then store them in tin or plastic boxes where they'll be protected against moisture and breakage. Kept dry, they'll keep for months. Enjoy the rocky crunch of rusk when your teeth crave it, or dunk pieces in coffee or soup to soften them.

Rose Honey

This recipe may seem terribly exotic for a boating cookbook, but the purpose of this chapter is to suggest ways you can bring a touch of home to your voyaging menus. This recipe takes the scent of your rose garden to sea.

8 ounces fragrant red rose petals, white trimmed away
2 cups water
2 pounds strained honey

Crush and bruise the rose petals well, then boil them in the water for 15 minutes. Add the honey and bring to a boil. Boil until the mixture is thick and syrupy, then strain it, pressing the rose petals well to get out all the honey. Return the honey to the pan and boil once more, then pour it into hot, sterilized jars and seal tightly. Serve on biscuits or toast.

⚓ Dilly Beans

Into each of four sterilized one-pint jars, place:

1 clove garlic, peeled
½ teaspoon mustard seed
½ teaspoon dried dill weed or one head fresh dill

Pack the jars tightly with well-washed, trimmed, whole green beans, carrot sticks, strips of zucchini, or other vegetables. Force in as many vegetables as possible because they will shrink during processing, but leave at least a half-inch space in the top of the jar.

Combine in a saucepan:

2½ cups water
2½ cups 5-percent acid vinegar
¼ cup pickling or non-iodized salt

Bring this to a boil, then pour over the vegetables, leaving half an inch of space in the top of the jar. Seal with canning lids, then place the jars in a large canner or pot, cover completely with water, and time ten minutes after the water has come to a boil. Do not eat for at least two weeks so flavor can develop fully.

20. COOKING THE CATCH

Adventures in catching, buying, and preparing all types of fresh seafood enrich the cruising diet as well as the cruising fun. If you plan to live off the sea, two books I've found extremely helpful are *Bottoms Up Cookery* by Leamer, Shaw, and Ulrich, published by Fathom Enterprises, and *Stalking the Blue-Eyed Scallop* by Euell Gibbons, published by David McKay Company. *The Edible Sea* by Paul and Mavis Hill, published by A. S. Barnes, is an invaluable guide to the collecting and preparing of all types of sea creatures and plants.

In addition to these books, it's important to get local knowledge about poisonous or dangerous sea groceries and native know-how about easy and delicious ways to attack the local product. Conch, for instance, is a one-minute project to the native who clunks the shell, removes the beast, and skins it with his teeth. Yet I've seen yachtsmen struggle for hours to do the same thing. In asking for help with handling your first catfish or butchering your first turtle, you'll make a friend while you learn tricks of the trade.

In this limited space I've concentrated on general recipes which will be successful with almost any fresh, firm, white fish from fresh or salt water.

Fish Saint Jacques

1½ pounds fish
¾ cup dry white wine
juice of 1 lemon
½ teaspoon salt
1 onion, minced
1 clove garlic, mashed
1 small can sliced mushrooms
¼ cup butter
⅓ cup flour
1 cup milk
a dash of nutmeg
2 tablespoons butter
1 cup soft bread crumbs

Cut the fish into walnut-size chunks, and poach it in the mixture of wine, lemon juice, and salt. When it's done, remove it from the liquid with a slotted spoon and portion it into six individual baking shells or arrange it in a single baking pan. Measure the cooking liquid, cool it, and add water if necessary to make one cup. Cook the onion, garlic, and mushrooms in the quarter-cup of butter until the onion is tender. Make a paste by stirring the milk gradually into the flour, then add this and the wine mixture to the hot onion mixture. Add the seasonings and cook, stirring, until it's smooth and bubbling. Spoon this mixture evenly over the poached fish. To bake in an oven, sprinkle the dish(es) with the bread crumbs, dot with butter, and bake ten minutes at 400°. If you're following stovetop directions (page 15), use the indirect method and omit the bread crumbs. After baking, add the crumbs after browning them in a skillet with the two tablespoons butter.

Paella *Svea*

Sue Moesly of *Svea* is one of the most inventive cooks I know, particularly in the use of spices. The next two recipes are hers.

1 large onion, diced
¼ cup butter
2 tablespoons fresh or dried green pepper
1 bay leaf
¼ teaspoon thyme
salt to taste
1 cup rice
2 cups water
1 one-pound can tomatoes
1 onion bouillon cube
1 vegetable bouillon cube
about 2 pounds firm white fish, cut into fingers

Sauté the onion in butter, then add the green pepper, rice, and herbs and coat thoroughly. Add the water, tomatoes, and bouillon cubes, cover, and simmer gently for 20 minutes. Add the fish fingers and cook, covered, ten minutes more or until the rice is tender. Makes six to eight servings.

Fish Fingers *Svea*

4 servings fish, in finger-size pieces
1 medium onion, diced
2 tablespoons butter
½ teaspoon curry powder
⅓ cup raisins
1 cup rice
2½ cups water
¾ cup sherry
1 can cheddar cheese soup
salt and pepper
a dash of Angostura bitters

209

Sauté the onion in butter, add curry, stir to coat, and then add the raisins and rice, stirring to coat them evenly. Add one cup of the water and stir to blend, then add the rest of the water and cover. Simmer 20 minutes. Add the sherry, fish, cheese soup, and seasonings and simmer over very low heat 15 minutes or more until the rice is tender.

🐚 Michigan Fish Boil

For this traditional Midwestern treat you need a very large kettle (about 12 quarts) plus a deep-fry basket which will fit into the pot.

For each crew member:

1 whole scrubbed potato
1 whole peeled onion
1 fish steak
2 cups salt (if you start with fresh water)

Have chopped parsley, melted butter, and lemon or lime slices on hand.

Put the potatoes into the pot with eight quarts sea water, or eight quarts fresh water plus one cup salt. Bring the water to a rolling boil, add the onions, bring to a rolling boil again, and cover. Boil steadily for 20 minutes, then add one more cup of salt if you're using fresh water, and a half-cup of salt if you started with sea water. Yes, you want a brine even stronger than the sea. The secret to keeping the foods from becoming too salty is to keep the pot always at a hard boil. Keeping it boiling, lower the basket with the fish steaks in atop the potatoes and onions, cover, and boil about ten minutes more. Test the fish to make sure it's done. Drain everything, and serve with butter, parsley, and lemon.

Thousand Islands Fish Fry

This is a time-honored routine which has evolved over the past century among fishing guides out of Clayton, New York. Cooked over a north woods fire, it is a delicious litany of one unusual course after another.

fat salt pork
sliced onions
fish
bread
ears of sweet corn
potatoes
eggs and milk for making French toast

Bring whole scrubbed potatoes to a boil in a large pot of water at the same time you are frying out the fat pork. This should not be smoked and should not contain lean. You'll need several pounds of it, diced. To fill their big, chuckwagon-size iron skillets, Clayton guides use five pounds of pork. After meat has been fried out, make sandwiches with the crisp pork, sliced raw onions, and fresh bread. Guests eat this while the chef continues. Keeping the fat very hot over a quick fire, place fish (steaks, fillets, well-scaled pan fish) in the fat at the same time as sweet corn is added to the boiling potatoes. When fish is crisp and corn has cooked for four or five minutes, this part of the meal is ready. Note that no flouring or seasoning has been used on the fish. All this is served with butter, lemon, and a big salad. Sometimes, if the catch has been meager, the guides grill T-bone steaks as the next course. The feast is finished with French toast. Make it with bread, milk, and eggs in the usual way, but deep-fry it in the sizzling-hot pork fat in which you cooked the fish. The taste is indescribably good and not at all greasy. This is traditionally served with a thimbleful of whiskey and maple syrup.

Fruited Fish

4 servings fish
2 tablespoons butter
½ teaspoon curry powder
½ cup grapefruit juice
2 large bananas

Cut up the fish into serving-size portions. Melt the butter in a large skillet, and stir in the curry powder. Add the fish, turn it to coat with the butter, then add the grapefruit juice. Cover and cook three to five minutes depending on the thickness of the fish. Cut the bananas in half lengthwise, then in halves, to make four pieces. Arrange the bananas and fish, turn each piece to coat, and cook, covered, a few more minutes until the fish flakes easily and the bananas are slightly softened.

Fisherman's Pie

4 servings fish
water
3 eggs
1 small can evaporated milk
salt and pepper to taste
freeze-dried chives to taste
6 tablespoons butter
1 one-pound can green beans
4 servings instant mashed potatoes, prepared according to
    package directions
bread crumbs

Poach the fish in water (or wine if you prefer) until it's just done. Drain it, break it apart, and mix it with two of the eggs, the milk, and the seasonings. Melt two tablespoons of the butter in a baking dish and add the green beans (well drained) and the fish. Add two tablespoons of the butter, melted, and the other egg to the mashed potatoes and mound them over the green beans and fish. Drizzle with the remaining butter and bake at 375° for 25 minutes or by the indirect Dutch oven method until everything is cooked through. Sprinkle with bread crumbs that have been fried in butter.

Deviled Fish

> 4 cups cooked fish
> 4 slices white bread
> 1 cup milk
> 3 tablespoons Worcestershire sauce
> 1 small onion, finely minced
> 1 tablespoon dried parsley
> salt and pepper to taste
> 1 teaspoon dry mustard
> cornflake crumbs and butter

Cut the crusts off the bread, soak the bread in the milk, and add the other ingredients except for the fish. Flake the fish and add it after cooking the milk mixture over low heat, stirring constantly, until it is smooth and thickened. Spread the mixture in a shallow casserole. For oven baking, sprinkle with cornflake crumbs, dot with butter, and bake 10 to 15 minutes at 350°. For the stovetop, use the indirect Dutch oven method and bake without the crumb topping until it's heated through. Then sprinkle with the crumbs after frying them in butter.

Wahoo One-Dish

This recipe originated with Captain Lee Bowring aboard the sportfishing charter boat *Sea Demon* out of St. Thomas. Except for the fresh fish, all the ingredients can be carried in your lockers.

1 medium onion, diced
2 tablespoons butter or oil
1 one-pound can of stewed tomatoes (preferably the type
    which includes green pepper and celery)
1 one-pound can sliced potatoes, rinsed and drained
McCormick fish seasoning
fresh fish in serving-size chunks

Sauté the onion in a little hot oil or butter, than add the remaining ingredients, cover, and simmer until the fish is done.

 Conch Egg Rolls

This recipe was developed by cruising sailor Carol Horowitz for use with conch. Flaked, cooked fish, crab, or shrimp can also be used if they are more common to your boating area. Making egg rolls is a long, multi-step job so it's one I save for days when I have plenty of time for cooking. The result is well worth the work, and the leftovers make delicious finger food, served cold.

Filling:

2 medium conchs (or 2 cups ground, cooked fish, shrimp,
    meat, etc.)
1 stalk celery
1 large onion
1 small can water chestnuts
salt and pepper to taste

⚓ Egg Roll Wrappers:

2 eggs
1 cup flour
2 teaspoons cornstarch
½ teaspoon salt
2 cups water

Chop or grind together the filling ingredients. Whisk together the wrapper ingredients to make a thin, smooth batter. Cook the wrappers in a skillet or crepe pan (see page 32 for instructions on cooking crepes) but cook on just one side. Turn them out, cooked side down, and stack between layers of paper toweling. Put a teaspoon of filling on the uncooked side of the wrapper, fold over one side, then fold in two sides, sealing with raw batter as you go. Fold over the last side, and seal again. Fry the rolls carefully in deep, hot oil until they are brown and crusty. Serve with bottled sweet-and-sour sauce or hot mustard.

Galley Tips: Fish

Tuck away in your lockers a few cans of clams in shells. They'll add a continental look to your paella.

Instead of dipping fillets into egg or milk before dredging in cornmeal or flour for frying, spread dried fillets with mayonnaise which has been mixed with a little Dijon mustard. Then dip in flour or crumbs.

If you plan to depend heavily on fresh fish for cruising meals, add a stovetop fish smoker which will give meals a change of pace. They're sold in gourmet and housewares stores.

To make an easy fish stew, simmer chunks of fresh fish in canned zucchini with tomato sauce.

Use slivers of hard salami to spice paella and other fish specialties. Many types carry for weeks without refrigeration.

Look for dehydrated horseradish in spice departments and specialty shops. Rehydrated with a little water, then mixed with ketchup, it makes a zingy cocktail sauce.

21. MAKE-AHEAD MIXES

To the voyager, making mixes ahead means that you save time, because you don't have to reach for a dozen canisters and boxes each day to combine the flours and ingredients you put into pancakes or biscuits. It also means that, instead of washing a bowl, spoon, pastry blender, and other gadgets each day, you make one big batch to last a week or so. Make the mixes in calm weather; in heavy weather you need only add water or do some other simple step.

To the weekender or boat camper, mixes make good sense, too, because they can be combined at home where you have a good selection of ingredients and herbs. They'll give you lots of variety in the galley without the need to carry box after bottle after jar of spices and staples. On many short cruises, I take no staples at all, and use mixes exclusively.

To every galley cook, make-ahead mixes mean a big savings in money and a chance to suit individual family yens for more cinnamon or less sugar. And mixes are of special value to the cook who likes to use whole grains, unusual flours, and minimal salt or sugar because commercial mixes are usually made with bleached flour, preservatives, and other ingredients which some people are trying to avoid.

On the minus side, homemade mixes can't be expected to keep as well as commercial ones because your own mixes don't contain stabilizers and preservatives. Don't make batches larger than you can use in a week or so, especially if the mixes contain fat. Keep them dry, and in the coolest spot possible.

🐾 Basic Biscuit Mix

8 cups flour
1½ cups nonfat dry milk
3 tablespoons baking powder
1 tablespoon salt
2 cups vegetable shortening

Combine the dry ingredients in a large bowl, mix well, and cut in the shortening until the mixture is mealy. Store in a well-sealed container and use it in any recipe that calls for Bisquick or biscuit mix.

🕊 Biscuits

3 cups basic biscuit mix
1 cup water

Mix with a fork just to moisten. Pat out on a floured cloth or paper towel and knead just until smooth. Flatten, then cut into circles or squares about half an inch thick. Bake on a hot griddle according to stovetop baking directions (page 16) or in a 425° oven until biscuits are browned.

Variations:

To make a shortcake base, add half a cup of sugar to this recipe and replace part of the water with an egg. Bake, split, and serve with fruit.

To make a coffee cake, add an egg and enough water to make a thick batter, spread in a square pan, top with streusel, and bake according to the indirect Dutch oven method until the cake is springy.

To make dumplings, add water to make a thick dough and drop by teaspoons onto boiling soup or stew. Boil ten minutes uncovered, then ten minutes tightly covered.

Streusel Topping Mix

1⅓ cups light brown sugar, packed
1 cup flour
2 teaspoons cinnamon
¼ cup sweetened hot cocoa mix (optional)
¾ cup butter

Combine the dry ingredients in a roomy bowl, then cut in the butter or margarine until the mixture is fine crumbs. Store it for up to a week in a tightly lidded container, and use it as a topping for coffee cake, canned fruit, pudding, or hot cereal.

Basic Pancake Mix

10 cups flour (white, buckwheat, whole wheat, barley flour, a little soy flour, or other grains as desired)
3⅓ cups nonfat dry milk
4 tablespoons baking powder
2 tablespoons salt

Mix well and package in plastic bags. To complete pancakes, use about a half-cup of mix per person. Add water, with an egg if you like, to make the batter thick or thin as you prefer. You may also add a tablespoon or two of salad oil or melted butter, but I often make pancakes with neither oil nor eggs. If you want sour milk pancakes, add a half-teaspoon of baking soda to each cup of the mix, and use sour milk or yogurt in place of the water. Bake on a very hot griddle, flipping after the top bubbles and the bottom browns.

Note: it isn't recommended that crepes be made with this mixture.
Variations: fold into the batter bits of ham, crumbled bacon, imitation bacon bits, chunks of apple, raisins, or banana slices.

Herbed Bread Crumb Mix

1 loaf white bread, dried and made into fine crumbs
⅓ cup dried onion flakes
⅓ cup dried parsley flakes
1 tablespoon seasoned salt
2 teaspoons MSG
1 teaspoon salt
¼ teaspoon pepper
1 teaspoon mixed Italian herbs

Mix everything together well and store it in a dry place in a well-lidded container. Use this in place of bread crumbs when you're making meatballs, or in tuna or salmon loaf. Use the mix as a coating for potato cakes and meat patties, and for dredging fish before frying. To make a tangy topping for vegetables, fry a few tablespoons of the mix in butter and sprinkle over hot cooked vegetables.

Pudding Mix

2 cups nonfat dry milk
1 cup sugar
¾ cup cornstarch
1 teaspoon salt

Mix everything together well and package in tightly sealed plastic bags. To make pudding, combine one and one-eighth cups of the mix with two cups cold water (or, for vanilla sauce, use a scant cup of mix). Bring to a boil, stirring over a very low heat, and cook until the mixture is smooth and thickened. Remove it from the heat and add a walnut-size nugget of butter and a teaspoon of vanilla. Pour into four paper cups or serving dishes, adding fruits or nuts if desired. For a flan effect, float a thin layer of caramel ice cream sauce on top. To make chocolate pudding, proceed as above but add two tablespoons of unsweetened cocoa to the dry mixture before adding the water.

⚓ Corn Bread Mix

4 cups flour
4 cups yellow cornmeal
2 cups nonfat dry milk
¾ cup sugar
¼ cup baking powder
1 tablespoon salt

Mix everything well and store it dry. For easy mixing, store the mix in batches of two and one-third cups in one-quart-size Zip-Loc bags. Force all the air from the bags and seal them well. To make corn bread, add an egg, a quarter-cup salad oil, and one cup water to the bag and work it with your hands just until the dry ingredients are evenly moistened. Strip the batter into the pan and bake in a 425° oven or according to indirect Dutch oven method until the bread is springy to the touch. For variety, add some blueberries or grated cheese to each batch.

Brandish (herbal)

¼ cup butter
3 cups All-Bran
1 tablespoon dried chopped onion
2 tablespoons grated cheese
1 teaspoon salt
1 teaspoon mixed Italian seasonings

Melt the butter and stir in the other ingredients. Spread into a baking pan and bake for ten minutes at 350°. Cool, then bottle tightly. Sprinkle brandish on salads, vegetables, or canned meats.

🐚 Brandish (sweet)

¼ cup butter
3 cups All-Bran
3 tablespoons grated orange rind
2 teaspoons pumpkin pie spice

Melt the butter and add the other ingredients. Bake it in a shallow pan at 350° or toss it in a skillet over low heat for ten minutes. After it's completely cool, package or bottle it tightly. Sprinkle sweet brandish on desserts, muffins, cake, pancakes, and puddings. Brandishes add both fiber and texture contrast to your cruising diet.

Rice Mixes

To each two cups of dry rice, add one of the following:

- 3 teaspoons dried, grated lemon peel
  2 teaspoons dill weed
  4 teaspoons granular chicken bouillon

- 1 envelope onion soup mix

- Spanish rice (when cooking the rice, use tomato sauce and water):
  ¼ cup dried bell pepper flakes
  2 teaspoons granular bouillon (beef, chicken, or vegetable)
  ½ teaspoon mixed Italian herbs

- 3 teaspoons dried, grated orange rind
  ¼ cup celery flakes
  4 teaspoons granular chicken bouillon

- ¼ cup raisins
  2 tablespoons curry powder (or to taste)
  2 tablespoons onion flakes
  4 teaspoons salt or granular bouillon (beef, chicken, or vegetable)

Package your mixes by the cupful in individual bags, well sealed. To make four servings, cook each cup of rice mix with two cups of water.

For a Basic Cream-Sauce Mix, see page 61. For Hot Drink Mixes, see pages 171 to 172.

Galley Tips: Mixes

The most convenient of all master mixes is self-rising flour, which is sold in many stores. It is flour, leavening, and salt to complete in any way you choose, from biscuits to waffles.

Bag individual batches of oatmeal with a variety of raisins, dried fruit, and nuts. For each serving, cook a half-cup mix with one cup water.

Make unusual, varied ready-to-eat cereal by combining several different boxes in a large container. Include some sugared cereals if you like them, some bran cereals, and different grains and shapes. Add nuts and raisins if desired. Mix well and store in tightly sealed containers.

Multiply any favorite recipe and bag it in individual batches. If mixture contains fat, don't make more than you'll use in a week or two unless you can refrigerate it.

Mixes make practical, welcome gifts to fellow cruising folk and to hostesses ashore, especially if there is a special blend your guests tell you is delicious and unusual. Include instructions for completing the mix.

Any mixes which call for eggs can be made with powdered eggs at the beginning. When reconstituting the mix, add more water.

22. ROUGH WEATHER AND RACING

When is it too rough to cook? On some boats it's when seas turn from satin to corduroy and the door of the front-opening icebox falls open. On other boats, cooking goes on with the cook strapped into the galley as spume spits in the Primus flame and the boat heaves through seas at a 45° heel.

Whether you are racing rail-down, caught in an unforecast squall, or are on a long passage where you have to take everything nature dishes up, your menus in heavy weather will be dictated in advance by how well the galley has been planned, by what foods you have on hand, and by where things are stowed.

Race cooks, knowing that they'll be busy with crew work and cooking as well, do most of their cooking ashore and just warm it up aboard. Cruising cooks can often assemble a quick, one-pot meal before a cold front hits. Voyaging cooks may even have enough time to bake several loaves of bread before encountering a forecast gale. Here are some suggestions for smoothing the cook's path through rough waters:

• I don't recommend cooking in an RV under way, even in a closed oven or crock pot. In a hard turn or panic stop, a casserole could crash against the oven door enough to open it. Too, an open flame is always a hazard on the highway. Even if your RV stays safe, you could happen onto an accident scene in which gasoline or propane is leaking.

• Have one special locker, preferably one which opens from the top so it can be opened no matter which way the boat is heeled or rolling, filled with nourishing finger foods. These include nuts, ready-to-eat dried fruits, individually wrapped pieces of cheese, fruit leather, granola bars, juices in flip-strip cans, single-serve fruits and puddings, jerky sticks, and perhaps a carton of hard-boiled eggs. Apples and other easy-to-eat fresh fruit can also be kept in this locker. There are times in almost every voyage when you can manage nothing more than these cold, quick energizers.

• Keep a vacuum bottle (unbreakable stainless steel, preferably) filled with boiling water. This can be used to make coffee, tea, hot cocoa, instant mashed potatoes, hot cereal, instant soup, and freeze-dried one-dish meals.

• Much has been written in the past about sealing meal portions into boilable bags before a voyage. Those who have the equipment can keep such foods on ice for up to three days or can freeze them in a galley freezer or on dry ice. Everything from pancakes to curry to plain rice can be put into these pouches and reheated in boiling fresh or sea water. Make individual portions, or bag enough to feed the entire crew. After bagging foods, while the plastic is malleable from the heat of the food, pile bags into a square box or form of some sort so they will freeze in a squared-off shape. They'll stow more compactly, and the closer together you can pack frozen foods, the longer they'll stay frozen.

• A pressure cooker is the safest pot to use underway whether or not you are cooking under pressure, because the lid locks on.

• If you have to heat water, use a closed tea kettle rather than an open pan. A closed kettle spills less (mine has been knocked across the galley without spilling more than a table-

spoon), retains heat better, and pours more safely. Avoid tea
kettles with lift-off lids, which allow spilling, and long spouts,
which can be broken off.

• Baby-food fruits and puddings are nutritious, no-addi-
tive, single-serving desserts in disposable containers.

• A heavy rubber lab-type apron is added protection
against scalds for the cook. Buy one from a scientific supply
house or make one from old foul-weather gear.

• Opened cans of main-dish foods such as spaghetti and
meatballs, baked beans, or macaroni and cheese can be heated
directly in the cans, in a closed pressure cooker, with a little
water. Wear oven mitts to handle the cans, and eat directly from
the tin.

• Food poisoning makes rough going far rougher. Don't try
to cook far in advance and hold foods without refrigeration, or
to keep foods day after day in an icebox. Bacteria begin to multiply in temperatures above 45° and under 140°.

• Cooking the meal in rough weather is only half the battle.
Serving and eating it are the important part, and these become
easier if you can corral each individual meal in a large tray-pan.
A biscuit pan or rectangular cake pan—something large enough
to hold a serving plate or bowl, a mug, and a fork—is ideal. Tuck
in some buttered bread and a napkin, and with one hand you
can serve each person in the cockpit. Yachting Tableware, which
has nonskid bottoms, holds its seat well in these pans. Many
yachties prefer the large vegetable bowls as plates in rough
weather, rather than the flat dinner plates.

Part IV

PROVISIONING

23. HOW TO PROVISION

In all my years of stocking galleys large and small, for trips long and short, I've continued to feel the same twinge of apprehension that all cooks-on-the-go feel: Will I forget some key item that ruins this cruise for my family? Will we go hungry? Will I overbuy so much that I waste food or, worse still, look foolish?

This section covers the simple rules of thumb I have followed in provisioning for different kinds of trips over the years. These are general guidelines that need to be adapted to everyone's special circumstances. Use them in concert with the recipes in this book and with other cookbooks as well. Somewhere in the following pages there is a provisioning plan that will work for you.

The Guess-and-By-Gosh Method

All of us cherish choice. We relish our right to browse the supermarket daily or weekly, buying according to special needs for entertaining, the season of the year, best buys, and a family's changing tastes and appetites. When you're provisioning for a weekend, a week, a month, or even longer in an area where supplies will be sparse or perhaps not available at all, flexibility and choice are as important as ever.

231

Many of us think of exact menus as tasks for professional dietitians in hospitals, prisons, and elementary schools. We dislike doing the work, and dislike having to eat beef stew on Tuesday night because the menu says so. Without some planning, however, it's possible to reach the end of your vacation with nothing left but foods that don't go together, or things the children won't eat.

I know one couple who limped in after a couple of months at sea with nothing left but canned corn. They'd been living on it for a week. Another cook, provisioning for a month, bought eighteen dozen eggs.

Somewhere between these extremes, there is a provisioning program I think of as an educated guess. It's based on how many meals per day you expect to eat, and what courses you expect those meals to include.

There are good reasons for refusing to regiment, and for keeping your options open. Many travelers find that their appetites dwindle at sea or at altitude, or in very hot climates. Others develop strange quirks and cravings.

Captain Lou Kennedy, whose cargo schooner was torpedoed during World War II, told me that he and his lifeboat crew craved fruits and juices but could barely force themselves to eat the corned beef that was aboard their lifeboat. Many others use up so many calories in the active, outdoor life that starches burn up at a rate no one dreamed possible.

The RV life can be a sedentary one, with modest caloric needs. Hiking and skiing involve vigorous exercise. Cruising and sailboat racing can involve a twenty-four-hour clock and can be a strenuous fight for survival.

Using very simple math, start with the number of days you want to provision for: seven, twenty-one, or whatever. Then ponder how many meals you will probably eat per day.

Perhaps you don't eat breakfast, but like a midnight snack. Some people enjoy a midmorning snack, a substantial tea, or a lengthy cocktail hour. Let's assume for now that you'll eat breakfast, lunch, dinner, and one other, lighter meal. Using the figure for the number of days you're provisioning for, you'll need, say, twenty-one breakfasts, twenty-one lunches, and so on.

I often plan in meal "units" or "credits." One unit is what is needed to feed my family one course of one meal. Say we need twenty-one breakfasts for two people. That's twenty-one main-dish units and twenty-one fruit or juice units.

So, for each two individual-serve boxes of cereal, I'd check off one breakfast main-dish unit, and two individual-serve cans of grapefruit juice would be one fruit unit. Or, two eggs, two toaster pastries, and two sausage patties would be one unit. Toss into your supermarket basket a packet of pancake mix that makes eight 4-inch flapjacks, and you have another unit. If you had a family of four, you'd need four eggs, pastries, and sausages, or two packets of pancake mix, to make one unit.

Lunch is a difficult meal to plan but, generally, I plan a "main-dish" unit such as canned tuna, a couple of ounces of cheese, or a hard-boiled egg, plus bread or crackers, a fruit unit, and a dessert unit such as a candy bar or a couple of cookies.

For twenty-one days you'd need twenty-one dinner meats, twenty-one starch courses, twenty-one vegetables, twenty-one salad units, and twenty-one dessert units. The size of a unit, of course, depends on the size of your crew, but often the planning is done for you by package labels, which tell you how many each can or package will serve.

I can meat for our own use. Even if you have a freezer, canning lets you have on hand meat that is already cooked and that is instantly ready, without thawing. And you don't have to worry about plugging in, or the freezer breaking down.

It's as easy as canning tomatoes, except that it takes longer and a pressure canner must be used. By doing my own canning, I can eliminate bone, fat, and fillers and end up with unseasoned meat that can be used in any dish we have a yen for. Boneless lamb chunks end up in stew or curry, beef chunks in stroganoff or chili, chicken thighs with dumplings, boneless turkey breast is served with stuffing and gravy made by thickening natural juices. Commercially canned meats, by contrast, may have large percentages of fat or gravy.

If you can boneless meat by the pint, you have a pound, or four 4-ounce servings, per jar. Half pints can hold a half-pound of ground meat. For larger families, use quart jars. Use widemouthed jars to can meatloaf or boneless roasts. Buy lean, boneless meat, but not expensive cuts, because the long, hot canning process will tenderize them.

For a sixty-day provision, a typical list (can or jar sizes depend on family size) might be:

20 cans/jars beef, ground beef, corned beef
10 cans/jars chicken or turkey
6 jars home-canned pork chunks
6 jars home-canned lamb chunks
3–4 commercially canned hams
10 cans tuna, salmon, mackerel

Remainder in unusual or treat meats such as chipped beef, tongue, Spam, pickled pigs' feet, sausages, or other meats your family enjoys. This list does not include breakfast and lunch meats like canned bacon, additional tuna and chicken for salad.

Generally, you'll need one egg per person per day (some will be needed for cooking even if you don't usually eat eggs for breakfast), a quart of milk or the nonfat dry milk equivalent per person per day, and at least a half-cup of flour per person per day, plus whatever other cereals, grains, or mixes you'll have on hand.

Foods that I carry in quantity, because they keep a long time and can be used in many different ways, include peanut butter and jelly (breakfast, snacks, lunch, desserts), rice (dinner starch dish, hot with milk and sugar for breakfast, rice pudding for dessert), honey (sweetener, bread spread, energizer by the teaspoon), sprouts, which can be grown fresh as you need them, and wheat kernels, which are a complete food, and can be served as a cooked cereal or ground into flour for bread.

Graham crackers, as many as you can keep fresh, are also a good addition. Make them into piecrust, or make melty dessert sandwiches with marshmallows and chocolate. Break plain graham crackers into a bowl of milk as a bedtime snack. Or just eat them plain when you have the munchies.

Extra vinegar and oil can be useful for making your own salad dressings. When you have surplus oil, you can splurge on deep-fried treats. Extra vinegar will be handy for pickling carrots, celery, and green beans as a substitute for salads when you're out of lettuce.

These are the foods I call fudge factors because they can be used in many ways to stretch, replace, or enhance other supplies.

For those readers who will be very dependent on stored supplies and a freezer, I recommend having a good supply of sugar, pickling salt, vinegar, and canning jars on hand. If the freezer or generator fails, you can save the food by canning, salting, or pickling it and by making jelly with any thawing fruit.

The Master List

NONFOOD ITEMS

Aluminum foil
Charcoal, lighter
Bar soap
Cleaner, nonabrasive
Detergent for dishes
Disinfectant/deodorizer spray
Disposable baking pans
Facial tissues
Food storage bags, wraps
Garbage bags
Insect sprays
Matches
Paper plates, towels, napkins, cups
Scourer, nonabrasive
Sponge
Toilet tissue

Note: This list does not include personal items such as shampoo and toothpaste.

BASIC STAPLES

Baking soda, powder*
Butter or margarine
Cocoa*
Coffee, tea, creamer
Eggs

---

*For shorter outings, I recommend using only mixes—not only commercial mixes, but things you put together yourself. This eliminates the need for a long list of spices, herbs, and other staples.

Flour*
Jelly, jam
Mayonnaise
Milk (long-life, powdered, fresh, canned)
Mustard, relish, ketchup
Oil
Pancake syrup
Pasta
Peanut butter
Raisins
Rice
Salt, pepper
Sugar, sugar substitute
Spices, extracts, flavorings*
Tomato sauce or paste
Vinegar
Yeast*

SOME RANDOM TIPS ON BUYING PROVISIONS

• Buy mixes that are as complete as possible. For example, pancake mixes are available that include milk and eggs, and need only water added. Others call for eggs, milk, and oil.

• Read labels. Not every food that comes in a box is a convenience food. Some require multiple steps, several bowls and appliances, and freezing or refrigeration.

• Don't set too much store by servings promised on labels. "Four ½-cup servings" of mashed potatoes may be a teenage boy's equivalent of one 2-cup serving. Serving sizes of retort pouch and freeze-dried meals are particularly skimpy.

• Individual-serve packets and cans cost more but help in three important ways. (1) They help in your planning. Six individual cans of juice or pudding are six portions. (2) They stay closed and fresh until eaten, with no worry about spoilage or leftovers. (3) They provide portion control so waste is minimized.

The Master Menu

Although I prefer provisioning for long trips by "units," as described previously, there are times when the trip is so short and the needs so exacting, I resort to a complete menu and shopping list. Many cooks use such a master menu for longer trips and voyages, too. In fact, some families love list-making and planning all winter as they look forward to their summer trips.

Here's how. Make up menus for seven days, three meals a day plus one snack meal (coffee break, midnight snack, hors d'oeuvres). Use recipes from this book if you like, choosing from those in Part Two, which are made completely with stowed foods, or from other sections if you will be using some bake-take foods, catching fresh seafood, or shopping along the way for native fruits and vegetables.

Take into account too any meals you usually have in restaurants. Voyagers must eat every meal aboard, under way. RV travelers, and boaters who cruise busy waterways, sometimes consider dining out to be an important part of the travel fun. Often, vacationers eat breakfast and lunch in, dinner out.

Your master menu may be far different from this very simple, rudimentary sample. You may use grander recipes and gourmet ingredients, more canned goods or perhaps a grilled meat every night, but the idea is the same.

Approach it in three columns: (1) the name of the dish, (2) a list of ingredients to buy for it, and (3) a list of any ingredients you're sure to have on hand, thanks to your Basic Staples list, for such a dish.

Example: Breakfast, Day One (2 persons)

Dish	Shopping	On Hand
Grapefruit	1 grapefruit	Sugar
Eggs poached in pizza sauce	2 eggs	Coffee
	1 can pizza sauce	Cream
Toasted English muffins	English muffins	Butter

Example: Lunch, Day One

Dish	Shopping	On Hand
Ham-and-cheese sandwiches	ham, cheese	Bread
	lettuce	Mustard
Potato chips	Potato chips	Mayonnaise
Pickles, olives	Pickles, olives	
Diet cola	2 diet colas	
Apples	2 apples	

Example: Dinner, Day One

Dish	Shopping	On Hand
Beef stew	½ lb. stew beef	Cornstarch
	2 potatoes	Onions
	4 carrots	Wine
Italian bread	1 loaf bread	Celery
Tossed salad	Tomatoes	Garlic
	Scallions	Butter
Red wine	1 bottle Burgundy	Lettuce
		Salad dressing
Canned peaches	1 can peaches	
Cookies	Butter cookies	

Notes:

Pick up baked goods when we get to Bay Village: Marie's, Main Street. Don't forget terrific brats from Wurst World, across from Marie's, for Tuesday dinner.

Try putting a dab of raspberry jam in each peach half and drizzle with crème de cassis.

As you continue with this list, you'll soon see that many shopping-list items will carry over. That package of English muffins from day one, for instance, might go into Eggs Benedict for breakfast the next day. The leftover Italian bread will make good French toast or sandwiches another day.

By listing the number of eggs, colas, apples, and so on in your shopping list, you'll be able to add them up at the end and know how many will be needed, at least as far as the master list is concerned.

Once you have a master menu, and tune it up through a few tries until it's ideal for your galley, tastes, and travel needs, you can continue using it forever. In fact, many families love traditions such as waffles every Sunday or bean soup and corn bread every Saturday night.

If you travel so much that such a menu would get tedious, make a two-week master menu, and it will probably be months before anyone realizes you're having curried chicken every other Tuesday night!

The menu can be varied even more if you are vaguer about recipes. You may, for instance, list "potatoes" to go with Friday night's "grilled fish." The potatoes could be mashed, baked, boiled, dilled, fried, stuffed, or scalloped. The fish could be salmon steaks one week, mahi-mahi the next, charcoaled one week, mesquite-grilled the next.

See the lists starting on page 246 for more master-menu ideas.

The Family Cruise

Feeding a family of four for a week or two without a freezer and without stopping at supermarkets every day is a puzzler for most city dwellers, and is a problem even for those farm cooks who have well-stocked larders at home but only empty shelves aboard a rental boat, condo, or RV.

This list has been a bonanza to me, both in stocking our own galleys—where I use it as a back-up and checklist—and in planning for a week or two in rental units.

The following charts are a composite, typical of lists used by bareboat-charter firms. They're ideal for boating, but are also good for stocking a ski- or seashore condo, rental RV, hunting or fishing lodge, or a mountain cabin.

You'll see immediately that there's too much food, because fresh fruit, meat, and vegetables are duplicated with canned foods. If you can spare space and budget for such duplication, it allows you more options at mealtime. If you're too tired to cook, open the beef stew. If you decide at the last minute to eat out, don't thaw the chicken. Extra canned goods are lifesavers in case your trip lasts longer than you planned. Even if you have to abandon them at the end of the stay, they have been cheap insurance.

First, go through this list and cross out items that you know you'd never use for your particular family or situation. Not everyone uses instant coffee, some people are allergic to mustard, and many people dislike artificially flavored drink mixes. Then go back and add items you know you'd miss if they weren't available, such as dessert mixes, more soups, and fresh potatoes in place of the various instants listed here.

Experts in provisioning bareboats use lists much like this one. Your list may be different, depending on whether you have more or less ice chest/refrigerator/freezer space, and whether you can reprovision more often. Too, this list is typical of Caribbean tastes, and for cold-weather roving you'll probably want more soups and hot drinks, fewer cold drinks.

Note also that there is enough fresh meat for every dinner, and some lunches and breakfasts. You may prefer to cut down on the amount to allow for more restaurant meals. Meat is expensive and can spoil quickly if you can't keep it cold, so I prefer to rely a bit more on canned meats or meat substitutes than this list allows.

If possible, arrive with all meat, and as many other items as possible, frozen. When we're provisioning at home, or are driving or flying directly to the destination, I ask the butcher to cut, package, and freeze meats for me in just the amounts needed.

Frozen milk and juices act as block ice, to help keep other cold foods cold. If you're provisioning at home, turn on the refrigerator the night before or prechill the icebox for several hours with ice. Then throw that ice away, and pack the cold box with frozen or well-chilled foods.

The following chart assumes a party of four, and reprovisioning after ten to twelve days. It does not include soft drinks, alcoholic beverages, or bar supplies, so make a separate list if you want these items aboard.

NONFOOD ITEMS

	7–8 Days	9–10 Days	11–12 Days	13–14 Days
Cleanser	1	1	1	1
Joy liquid	1	2	2	3
Garbage bags (35-gallon)	6	7	8	10
Baggies	6	7	8	10
Off (insect repellant)	1	1	1	1
Insect spray	1	1	1	1
Aluminum foil (75 feet)	1	1	1	1
Matches	10	10	10	10
Paper towels	2	3	4	4
Toilet tissue	2	3	4	4

	7–8 Days	9–10 Days	11–12 Days	13–14 Days
Table napkins (90 count)	2	2	3	4
Kleenex, large	1	1	1	1
Bar soap	2	2	4	4
Charcoal	6	8	10	12
Scouring pad	1	1	2	2
Pot holder	2	2	2	2
Sponge	2	2	2	2
Paper plates	30	40	50	60
Paper cups	30	40	50	60

NONPERISHABLE FOOD

	7–8 Days	9–10 Days	11–12 Days	13–14 Days
Tuna, 6 oz.	2	2	4	4
Sandwich spread, 8 oz.	1	1	1	1
Mustard, 6 oz.	1	1	1	1
Mayonnaise, 8 oz.	1	2	3	3
A.1. sauce, 5 oz.	1	1	1	1
Worcestershire sauce, 5 oz.	1	1	1	1
Spaghetti sauce, 16 oz.	1	1	2	2
Chow mein noodles, 3 oz.	1	1	2	2
Beef chow mein, 16 oz.	1	1	2	2
Saltines, 1 lb.	1	1	2	2
Butter cookies, 1 lb.	1	2	3	3
Ritz crackers, ½ lb.	2	2	2	3
Iced tea, 1 qt.	4	4	6	8
Kool-Aid, 1 qt.	4	4	6	8
Evaporated milk, 13 oz.	1	2	2	2
Coffee creamer, 6 oz.	1	1	2	2
Tang, 2 qts.	2	2	4	4
Salt, pepper (disposables)	1	1	1	1
Seasoned salt	1	1	1	1
Black pepper	1	1	1	1
Nonfat dry milk, 1 qt.	4	4	6	8
Instant rice, 7 oz.	2	2	4	4
Mashed potatoes, 3 servings	3	3	6	6
Thin spaghetti, 1 lb.	2	2	4	4
Macaroni and cheese, 7 oz.	4	4	8	8
Coffee, ground	1	2	3	4
Coffee, instant	1	1	2	2
Tea bags, 16 count	2	3	4	4
Sugar, 1 lb.	1	1	1	2
Individual cereal, 12-pack	2	2	4	4
Spam, 12 oz.	2	2	4	4
Corned beef hash, 15 oz.	2	2	3	3

243

	7–8 Days	9–10 Days	11–12 Days	13–14 Days
Vienna sausage, 5 oz.	2	2	4	4
Beef stew, 15 oz.	2	2	4	4
Spaghetti and meatballs, 15 oz.	2	2	4	4
Canned ham, 2 lbs.	2	2	3	4
Mushrooms, 6 oz.	1	1	2	2
Tomato soup, 10½ oz.	2	2	2	2
Chicken broth, 10½ oz.	2	2	2	2
Consomme, 10½ oz.	2	2	2	2
Onion soup, 10½ oz.	2	2	2	2
Beets, 16 oz.	2	2	2	2
Mixed vegetables, 16 oz.	2	2	2	2
Peas, 16 oz.	2	2	4	4
Green beans, 16 oz.	2	2	4	4
Sweet corn, 16 oz.	2	2	4	4
Pork and beans, 16 oz.	2	2	4	4
Carrots, 16 oz.	2	2	4	4
Tomatoes, 16 oz.	2	2	4	4
Asparagus, 16 oz.	2	2	4	4
Whole potatoes, 16 oz.	2	2	4	4
Potato salad, 16 oz.	2	2	4	4
Syrup, 12 oz.	2	2	4	4
Peanut butter, 12 oz.	1	1	1	2
Grape jelly, 10 oz.	1	1	1	1
Strawberry preserves, 10 oz.	1	1	1	1
Orange marmalade, 10 oz.	1	1	1	1
Date-nut roll, 8 oz.	2	2	4	4
Fruit cocktail, 16 oz.	2	2	4	4
Apricots, 16 oz.	1	1	2	2
Sliced pineapple, 16 oz.	2	2	3	3
Purple plums, 16 oz.	1	1	2	2
Pears, 16 oz.	1	1	2	2
Fried onions, 4 oz.	2	2	3	4
Potato sticks, 4 oz.	2	2	3	4
Peanuts, 4 oz.	2	2	3	4
Ketchup, 14 oz.	1	1	1	1
Salad dressing, 8 oz.	1	1	2	2
Cocktail onions, 4 oz.	1	1	1	1
Sweet pickles, 8 oz.	1	1	1	1
Dill pickles, 8 oz.	1	1	1	1
Stuffed olives, 5 oz.	1	1	1	1
Vinegar, 12 oz.	1	1	1	1
Lemon juice, 8 oz.	1	1	1	1
Orange juice, 1 pt.	3	5	6	8

	7–8 Days	9–10 Days	11–12 Days	13–14 Days
Grapefruit juice, 1 pt.	3	5	6	8
Pineapple juice, 1 pt.	3	5	6	8
V-8 juice, 1 pt.	3	5	6	8
Wesson oil, 16 oz.	1	1	1	1
Liverwurst, 5 oz.	2	2	4	4
Shrimp, 7 oz.	2	2	2	4
Sardines, 4 oz.	2	4	4	6
Spreadables, 4 oz.	2	4	4	6

FRESH FOOD

	7–8 Days	9–10 Days	11–12 Days	13–14 Days
Gruyere cheese, 6 oz.	1	1	1	1*
Baby Gouda, 7 oz.	1	1	1+1*	1+1*
American-cheese slices, 8 oz.	2	3	3	2+2*
Bologna, 8 oz.	2	3	3	2+2*
Lunch meat, 8 oz.	1	1	1+1*	1+1*
Salami, 8 oz.	1	1	1	1+1*
Butter, ½ lb.	6	8	6+4*	6+6*
Eggs, 1 doz.	4	4	4+2*	4+4*
Bread	4	6	4+2*	4+4*
Apples	8	12	8+4*	8+8*
Oranges	8	8	8+4*	8+8*
Grapefruit	4	6	4+2*	4+4*
Limes	4	6	4+4*	4+4*
Cucumbers	2	4	4+2*	4+4*
Lettuce	4	4	4+2*	4+4*
Onions	4	6	4+3*	4+4*
Tomatoes	6	8	6+3*	6+6*
Fruit, other	2	2	2	2
Baking potatoes	4	4	8	12

FROZEN FOOD

	7–8 Days	9–10 Days	11–12 Days	13–14 Days
Lamb chops, 5–6 oz.	4	4	4	4
Pork chops, 5–6 oz.	–	4	4	4*
Beef tenderloin, 8 oz.	4	4	4	4
Strip loin steak, 8 oz.	–	4	4	4*
Chicken, whole	2	2	2	2+2*
Beef patties, 8 oz.	6	6	6+6*	6+6*
Beef wieners, 1 lb.	1	1	1+1*	1+1*
Bacon, 1 lb.	2	2	2+2*	2+2*
Sausage, 1 lb.	2	2	2+1*	2+2*
Milk, 1 qt.	4	4	4+3*	4+4*
Steak kabobs, 8 oz.	4	4	4	4+4*

*Reprovision

TYPICAL MENUS USING THESE FOODS

ARRIVAL-DAY DINNER
> Crackers, cheese, cocktails
> Charcoal-grilled steak with mushrooms
> Lettuce-and-tomato salad, dressing
> Peas with French-fried onions
> Baked potatoes
> Fresh fruit
> Coffee, tea

FIRST BREAKFAST
> Juice
> Eggs (hard-boil extras for sandwiches)
> Bacon
> Dry cereal with fresh milk
> Toast, jam
> Coffee

FIRST LUNCH
> Sandwiches
> Pickles
> Fresh fruit
> Iced tea, etc.

FIRST DINNER
> Mixed nuts with cocktails
> Barbecued chicken
> Instant rice with stuffed olives
> Green beans
> Fruit salad (canned fruit plus fresh)
> Cookies
> Coffee, etc.

SECOND BREAKFAST
Fresh grapefruit
Scrambled eggs with sausage
Cereal, milk
Toast, jam
Coffee

SECOND LUNCH
Bacon, lettuce, and tomato sandwiches
Potato sticks, pickles
Fruit
Drinks

SECOND DINNER
Grilled beef patties
Pan-browned onions
Mixed vegetable salad, dressing
Canned pears
Cookies
Drinks

THIRD BREAKFAST
Juice
Cheese omelet with Spam
Cereal with milk
Toast, jam, jelly
Coffee

THIRD LUNCH
Sandwiches
Relishes
Fruit
Drinks

THIRD DINNER
Peanut-butter-and-bacon canapes with cocktails
Grilled lamb chops
Buttered corn
Instant mashed potatoes
Asparagus and sliced-egg salad
Coffee, tea

FOURTH BREAKFAST
Juice
Corned beef hash with eggs
Cereal with milk
Toast, jam, jelly
Coffee

FOURTH LUNCH
Hot dogs
Canned beans
Cold drinks

FOURTH DINNER
Cheese and crackers with cocktails
Charcoal-grilled steak kabobs
Pan-browned canned potatoes
Tossed salad
Fruit
Coffee

FIFTH BREAKFAST
Juice
French toast with syrup
Cereal with milk
Coffee

FIFTH LUNCH
> Grilled cheese sandwiches
> Pickles
> Fruit
> Drinks

FIFTH DINNER
> Crackers, cheese, cocktails
> Charcoal-grilled tenderloin
> Macaroni and cheese
> Salad made from chopped apple, canned pineapple, peanuts
> Cookies
> Coffee, tea

SIXTH BREAKFAST
> Juice
> Omelet with chopped leftover ham
> Cereal with milk
> Toast, jam, jelly
> Coffee

SIXTH LUNCH
> Tuna-salad sandwiches
> Pickles
> Fruit
> Cold drinks

SIXTH DINNER
> Peanuts with cocktails
> Charcoal-grilled pork chops
> Mashed potatoes
> Green vegetable
> Sweet-and-sour beet salad
> Canned fruit
> Coffee

How Far Will It Go?

While it's easy enough to figure how many eggs you'll need at one per person per day, or to plan nonfat dry milk by the packet at the rate of a pint of milk per person daily, other foods and supplies are used so slowly that it's very hard to know how long they will last.

How many squeezes do you get from a 6.4-ounce tube of toothpaste? How many cups from a 10-ounce jar of instant coffee? How many splashes from a medium-size bottle of after-shave lotion? Squirts from a 16-ounce container of dishwashing detergent? Cups from a 4-pound box of Tide? Showers from a bath-size bar of Shield?

If you're planning a long provisioning project, such as packing supplies into a cabin in Alaska to last out the winter or stuffing a boat for a circumnavigation, it will help in your planning if you start months, perhaps even a year, in advance to keep notes on how long things last in normal usage.

When you open a fresh bottle, jar, or package, enter the item and date on a note sheet. When it's gone, add the date. By the end of six months or a year, you'll have a very good idea of how many tubes of toothpaste or jars of basil you go through in that amount of time.

The Ration

This method of provisioning is the least popular of all but some voyagers do use it. The device is less shocking to anyone who has ever been on a diet, or in the armed services.

The idea is simply to put yourself on an allowance of so-many this or that per meal or per day. Say you'll allow your-self one paper plate per person per day for lunch, but are forcing yourself to wash dishes after breakfast and dinner. So you buy one paper plate per person per day. I heard once of a boat on which each person was allowed so-many squares of toilet tissue per day. One of our cruising friends sliced paper-towel rolls in half, and allowed himself a half towel per use. Allot one vitamin C pill per day, one Butterfinger bar, two marshmallow cookies, one egg, one quart of milk, or what-ever. Be forewarned, however, that while this system results in closer planning and better sharing, it can also lead to mu-tiny.

To Help in Your Planning . . .

Can-Size No.	Weight	Cups	Approximate Servings
¼	4–4¼ oz.	½	1
½	8 oz.	1	2
1	10–13 oz.	1¼	2–4
303		2	3–4
2	1 lb. 2 oz.–1 lb. 8 oz.	2½	3–5
2½	1 lb. 10 oz.–2 lb. 3 oz.	3½	4–6
3	2 lbs.	4	5–8
10	6–8 lbs.	12–13	24–26 of ½ c. each
1 tall		2	
13 fl. oz. evaporated milk	14½ oz.	1⅔ c.	

CEREALS

Barley, quick   ¼ c. plus water = ¾ c. (1 serving)
Cornflakes   1 c. crushed = ¼ c. crumbs
Cornmeal   1 c. plus 5–6 c. water (to taste) = 4+ cups
Crackers, graham   18 crushed crackers = 1 c. crumbs
Cream of Wheat   ⅔ c. = 3 c. cooked or 3 1-c. servings
Flour, graham   1 lb. = 4–4½ c.
Flour, instant   2 lbs. = 7–7½ c.
Flour, rye   1 lb. = 4½–5 c.

DRIED FRUIT AND SHELLED NUTS

Pecans	1 lb. = 3–4 c.
Prunes	1 lb. = 10–13 servings
Raisins	1 lb. = 2⅔ c.
Walnuts	1 lb. = about 4 c.

MISCELLANEOUS

Eggs, powdered	2 T. plus 2 T. water = 1 whole egg
Eggs, powdered whites	1 T. plus 2 T. water = 1 fresh egg white
Eggs, powdered yolks	1½ T. plus 1 T. water = 1 fresh egg yolk
Lemons	1 lb. (3–5) = 1 c. juice
Milk, powdered	1⅓ c. + water = 1 qt.
	4–5 lbs. = about 20 qts. (brands differ)

SEEDS FOR SPROUTING	AMT. NEEDED PER QT. OF SPROUTS
Alfalfa	3 T.
Fava	1 c.
Garbanzo	1 c.
Lentils	¾ c.
Mung beans	¾ c.
Soybeans	1 c.
Sunflower seeds	1 c.
Wheat	1 c.

Emergency Foods

No matter how short the distance you're going, or brief the time you plan to spend on the go, I recommend having extra food and water on hand. For a day's outing, that could be a few cans of juice and peanuts. For a week, have a full day's extra provisions. For longer provisioning have at least one extra day's rations for each week you'll be gone.

You could be delayed by any number of things: a bridge that is stuck shut so you can't get your sailboat into port, a grounding, mechanical failure in your boat or RV, a road washout that keeps you from leaving your hunting lodge on schedule, or even something as prosaic as a lost kitten. We once knew a family whose cat got lost on a deserted island and they stayed on for three increasingly hungry days before they found him. Food and water are cheap insurance.

The foods you stow away for emergencies needn't be gourmet fare but they should be easy to prepare with little fuel and water, and should provide as much nourishment as possible. They should also have a long shelf life, so you can put them away and forget them until needed.

SUGGESTED ONE-DAY EMERGENCY MENU

1 tin imported Scottish oats (sold in gourmet food
    departments)
Dry or long-life milk
Jar artificial orange-juice powder
1 tin crackers (gourmet food department)
Jar peanut butter or can tuna
1–2 cans fruit
1 jar processed cheese
Canned complete main dish such as beef stew,
    chow mein, chili, hearty soup, or tuna with noodles
Jars pickles, olives
Tin Boston brown bread
Drink mix such as lemonade

Emergency Company Meals

Not all emergencies involve delays, breakdowns, and other headaches. Sometimes there's a happy reason for delving into your cache of emergency supplies—for example, to stretch a meal to include strangers. We once sailed into a marina in the Bahamas and were delighted to find old friends had made an unscheduled stop there. It was somebody's birthday or anniversary, so I rummaged around in my goodies locker and rustled up a quick and festive meal for four.

Another time, we were camping in a state park where a very unusual, foreign-built camper caught our eye. We went over to snoop, discovered that the couple aboard were Swiss tourists who were spending two years exploring North America, and we invited them to dinner. Although I had provisioned only for two, my emergency shelf pulled us through again.

Here are some dishes that can be pulled together out of supplies saved just for such emergencies. I keep them together, in a separate bag or box if possible, so I always have the makings of a complete, balanced, and pretty meal. Usually, of course, there are fresh foods on hand, too, which can be substituted for, or added to, these stowed ingredients.

BREAKFAST

Stow: canned juice or nectar, grapefruit sections, or canned, cooked prunes.

Lemon Short Stack. Stow: 1 can lemon-pie filling, 1 box complete pancake mix, 1 can bacon. Fry bacon separately. Make big, thin pancakes, adding an extra egg or two if you have them. Spread lemon-pie filling lavishly between pancakes as you stack them. Cut stack into pie-shaped wedges to serve. With lemon filling, you don't have to wonder if you have enough syrup and butter.

LUNCH

If you always have plenty of fresh bread on hand to make sandwiches, lunch is less a problem, but there is no real substitute for it. So, if you need an emergency lunch and are out of bread, you might serve:

Pumpkin Soup (page 88). Stow: 2 cans pumpkin, extra quart-size envelope nonfat dry milk. (Seal in a freezer-type plastic bag to protect freshness; watch expiration date.) Have on hand brown sugar, salt, butter, cayenne.

Carr's Table Water Crackers (found in import section of supermarket), and:

1 jar Old English style cheese
Or 1 package bread sticks (watch expiration date)
Canned pineapple chunks in natural juice for dessert

DINNER

Beer Bread (page 114). Stow: 1 can beer. Have on hand: self-rising flour. This is a quickie, but the smell of fresh bread will wow your guests.

Or 1 package hot-roll mix (watch expiration date).

Small jar honey (use as a spread if you find you're out of butter or margarine).

1-lb. can baby whole carrots or whole Blue Lake green beans. Drain, rinse, drain again. Have on hand: Italian dressing or vinegar, oil, and herbs. Marinate vegetables as long as possible. Serve as a salad.

Or 1 can tomato aspic. All you do is slice and serve. (Chill if there is time.)

Schnitz and Knepp (page 53). Stow: 1½ lb. canned ham, 1 can pie-sliced apples, 1 or 2 packets biscuit mix (watch expiration date). Have on hand: brown sugar.

Or Chop-Chop Suey (page 53). Stow: two 6-ounce cans chunky chicken or 1 pint home-canned boneless chicken; 2 cans mixed Chinese vegetables. Have on hand: fresh onion, cornstarch, sherry, bouillon, Gravy Master. Stow: small box or bag rice to serve with this.

A bottle of wine will cheer up this meal.

For dessert, Downey's cake. Sold in gourmet departments of larger department stores, these cakes weigh more than two pounds, have a shelf life of at least a year, and are available in six luscious flavors, including Kahlúa, piña colada, and chocolate mint. Cost is about $25 per cake, but this is truly a celebration dessert and it stays fresh until you need it.

Substitutions

Baking powder, per teaspoon = ¼ t. soda plus ⅝ t. cream of tartar; or ¼ t. soda plus ½ c. sour milk or ¼ t. soda plus ¼ to ½ c. molasses. (Decrease other liquids correspondingly if sour milk or molasses are added.)

Butter, per cup = 7 oz. oil or 7 oz. shortening

Buttermilk = substitute yogurt cup for cup.

Coconut milk, substitute regular milk cup for cup and add up to ½ t. coconut flavoring. Substitute cream cup for cup for coconut cream, and use artificial coconut flavor.

Cornstarch, for thickener, per T. = 2 T. flour or 2 t. arrowroot. In a pinch you can also use dried potato flakes or tapioca as a thickener.

Chestnuts are often substituted for in the West Indies by breadfruit seeds. Ask for local knowledge.

Chocolate, baking. One ounce = 3 T. cocoa plus 1 T. butter or margarine.

Flour, all-purpose, per cup = 1 c. less 2 T. cornmeal; or 1 c. graham or rye flour; or 1⅔ c. bread crumbs; or 1 c. oatmeal

Herbs, 1 T. fresh = about ½ t. dried. Do not substitute dried basil for fresh in pesto.

Sour milk, cream. 1 t. lemon juice or vinegar per cup of milk or cream will create the sour taste and consistency needed in most recipes.

Sugar, granulated, per c. = 1⅓ c. brown sugar; or 1½ c. confectioners sugar; or 1½ c. corn syrup, with corresponding reduction in liquid in recipe. Or 1 c. honey, omitting ⅓ c. liquid, or 1⅓ c. molasses, omitting ⅓ c. liquid.

Whipped cream, 2 c. = 1 c. instant dry milk plus 1 c. ice water; beat; add ¼ c. lemon juice and fold in ½ c. sugar.

When traveling in other countries you'll almost always be dealing in metrics and, in England or in nations where British-made stoves are used, oven temperatures are given in Regulo numbers.

U.S.	British	Metric
quart	1½ pints +	scant liter
1 pint	approx. ¾ pint	scant demiliter
½ cup	3–4 oz.	deciliter +
1 oz.	1 oz.	approx. 28 grams
8 oz.	8 oz.	approx. 227 grams
pound +	pound +	500 grams
approx. 2¼ lbs.	approx. 2¼ lbs.	1 kilogram

There's no need to memorize any conversion tables or do complicated math. As you shop, keep in mind that a "kilo" of meat or vegetables is about 2¼ pounds. Because a kilogram is 1,000 grams, you can easily ask for 500 grams if you want a pound of meat or 225 grams if you want about half a pound of cheese.

As you cook, you can forget conversions completely because your galley or kitchen will probably be equipped with metric measuring devices and cookbooks. A recipe will ask for, say, a deciliter of milk, which you pour into a measuring cup that is marked in metrics.

In most countries, milk is sold by the liter, which is a little more than a quart. In Britain and countries where British products are sold, milk is usually sold by the Imperial pint, which is about 3 cups.

Oven temperatures are

Regulo	F.	C.
1	290	143
2	310	154
3	335	168
4	350	176
5	375	190
6	400	204
7	425	218

Food Safety

"When in doubt, throw it out." The old housewives' adage is twice as meaningful for the cook-on-the-go because you and your family are often miles away from medical help. Food poisoning, even when it is not life threatening, is painful and debilitating.

Refrigeration, the modern miracle that now travels with us, can be a mixed blessing, because the absorption-type refrigeration used in most campers and boats is not as efficient as the compressor units we have at home. Therefore, we can be left with a false sense of security.

In very hot weather, such units simply can't cope, because most of them can achieve only a 40- to 50-degree drop from ambient temperatures. On a 95-degree day, your refrigerator may run as warm as 50 degrees. If you overwhelm the refrigerator with too many warm foods at once, it can't keep up even on cool days.

If you have a compressor unit, and try to get by with less engine or generator time, temperatures can rise into the danger range, too.

Organisms that cause food poisoning grow most rapidly at temperatures above 45 degrees and below 125 degrees. Start with fresh foods, clean hands, and clean working conditions. Then simply keep cold foods cold, and hot foods hot—140 degrees or more—and you're almost certain to be safe.

The only way to be sure your foods are cold enough is to use a refrigerator thermometer. The cheapest ones cost only about a dollar in hardware and home stores, and have the "safe" refrigerator range clearly marked. For a little more money you can get a thermometer that mounts on the outside, with a probe to place inside. With this type, you always know food temperatures at a glance without opening the refrigerator door.

The most common food poisons are Salmonella, which occurs most commonly in raw meat and dairy products; Clostridium perfringens, found in high-protein foods; and staph, which is spread by infected people to such host foods as potato salad. Botulism, which is the most deadly poison of all, is fairly rare, so it's probably the least of your problems.

Here are some additional food safety tips:

• Keep canned drinks, and other noncritical items, in a separate ice chest. Every time the refrigerator door is opened and closed, heat enters. By keeping drinks separate, a lot of traffic is eliminated.

• Prechill a refrigerator or freezer before provisioning. When adding a great many supplies at once, buy them cold or frozen if possible. If you use an ice chest, prechill it first with sacrificial ice, discard, then fill with fresh ice and cold food.

• Dry ice can be a help, but use it with caution. Don't touch it with bare hands. Protect foods from it with several layers of newspaper, or freezer burn results. Don't use dry ice to chill carbonated beverages. They can explode. Don't use large quantities of dry ice in a small cabin without adequate ventilation. It "melts" as carbon dioxide.

• Don't let the kids dip into foods with a utensil that has been in someone's mouth.

• Use covers to keep flies from lighting on food.

• In boating and camping it's best to throw leftovers away.

• When you don't have a dishwasher, unlimited running water, and other aids, you have to work twice as hard at cleanliness. Use a small brush to clean the can opener blade and other small, recessed areas where food bits can lurk. Wood cutting boards trap food particles, too. A mild bleach solution will help sanitize wood items.

• Keep family members who have skin infections or colds away from the galley.

• Never cook food partially at home, to be completed on board. Keep it cold and raw, cooked and chilled, or cooked and hot.

Packaging for Freshness

Most foods are provided by their producers with the packaging that will keep them freshest and most tasty until you eat them. Still, in cooking on the go we're faced with more temperature and humidity extremes, jiggling, and sometimes stretching out storage times well beyond recommended limits.

Here are some ways to package stowed foods better:

• Cut the ribbed tops from crew socks that are worn out heel and toe. The tops are still good. Slip them over glass bottles to cut down on clanking and breakage.

• Many brands of soft drinks, salad oil, peanut butter, vinegars, and other products are available in plastic.

• Frozen foods will taste better longer if you encase them in an additional layer of freezer wrap or double-bag them in plastic.

• For very-long-term keeping, buy staples in enameled cans from reserve food stores (see **Dehydrated Foods** in Glossary).

• Keep cans from rusting by coating them, labels and all, with clear lacquer spray. Or seal each can in a plastic bag. Or paint with melted wax.

• Aluminum cans and aluminum foil corode very quickly in a salt atmosphere. Keep them as dry as possible.

• Where cans have lift rings (corned beef hash, Vienna sausages, single-serve puddings), tape them down. They can be jostled under way and the seal broken.

• Some foods are exceedingly hygroscopic (they absorb moisture out of the air). Among them are chocolate cocoa mixes, freeze dried foods, instant coffee and tea, and artificial fruit-drink mixes. Add additional wrapping or bagging; don't open manufacturer packing until you're ready to use. Buy in small sizes; use quickly.

• Although some on-the-go cooks try to avoid buying products in glass bottles, glass is a far better moisture barrier than is plastic. For long-term keeping, glass is best.

• For very-long-term storage, any grain products should be protected against infestation. (Eggs may already be in the product when you buy it.) You might seal the product very well in several layers of plastic and then freeze it for twenty-four hours. Thaw without opening. Or pack it into an airtight can in which you've first placed a nugget of dry ice. Let it vent for a few minutes, then seal. The CO_2 should kill any livestock that has stowed away.

• Favor those products that have expiration dates you can read, rather than codes that only the supermarket can decipher.

• Use a marking pen to date all goods that come into the galley so you can use older foods first.

• If any canned product looks or smells bad, throw it away without tasting.

• Specialty and gourmet shops often sell imports in tins that we don't usually buy in tins, such as oatmeal, marmalade, syrups, crackers, cookies, cakes, and candies. For long-term provisioning, the added cost is often worth it.

• Fresh lettuce and other delicate produce keep longer if wrapped in paper toweling or clean terry cloth. Although many voyaging cooks use newspaper, I don't recommend it because of the chance of contamination by printers' ink.

• If you wash and bag salad greens at home, to carry in your galley refrigerator for a day or two, dry well, then seal in a plastic bag with lots of air. This cushions the greens against squashing as foods shift under way.

For more food-packaging tips, see Glossary.

GLOSSARY
(AND ASSORTED TIPS)

Apples. Buy hard, fresh, unbruised fruit early in the season. Wash, and wrap the pieces individually in brown paper or paper toweling (not foil or plastic). Apples will keep up to several months depending on temperatures, bruises, and the original state of the apples at purchase. Also available canned or dried.

Bacon. In supermarkets you will find canned bacon, canned crumbled bacon, and imitation bacon bits. Cured bacon needing no refrigeration is sold by specialty stores and mail-order houses (see *Ham*). Camping suppliers sell specialty packs. Fresh vacuum-pack bacon is dated for keeping in the refrigerator.

Bananas. Buy them as green as possible and the supply will last some weeks. Banana flakes are sold in some markets, and dehydrated bananas sold by reserve food stores.

Butter, margarine. Available fresh, canned, and dehydrated. If you pack fresh, regular margarine (not whipped or soft) in scalded plastic containers and keep it away from excessive heat, it will last for weeks.

Cabbage. Buy fresh hard heads and remove any cellophane wrap. Allow cabbage to breathe, keep it from bruising, and keep it away from excessive heat. Use leaves from the outside, working in. (Don't cut through the head; the outer leaves continue to protect the inner leaves.) Lasts several weeks.

Carrots. Bagged supermarket varieties last only a few days without ice, but fresh farm carrots, unwashed and kept cool, will

265

last longer. Allow them to breathe. Shop for canned carrots in a variety of shapes: diced, sliced, shredded, and baby whole. Available dehydrated.

Cheese. Many varieties will •keep without refrigeration. Shop the supermarket, where you'll find cheese spreads in jars and squirt cans, in foil-wrapped wedges, and in boxes (Velveeta). Lasting qualities are very good before the packages are opened. To keep large cheeses after cutting them, wrap the cut end in vinegar-soaked cheesecloth. Dehydrated and freeze-dried cheeses are available in long-life tins. Shop locally for unrefrigerated cheese, and ask for the best-keeping whole cheeses at specialty shops. Order specialty cheese from Cheese of All Nations, 153 Chambers St., New York NY 10007.

Chutney. Like other relishes, this keeps a week or more after opening.

Coconut. In the tropics, carry unopened coconuts. You can buy grated or shredded coconut in cans and packages. Cans keep best for the long term. Commercial coconut cream is also available in cans, usually with bar supplies.

Corn syrup. Keeps indefinitely on the shelf.

Cottage cheese. Check camping suppliers for Mountain House brand freeze-dried cottage cheese.

Dehydrated foods. To find dehydrated foods in enameled, long-life tins, look in the Yellow Pages under "Foods–Dehydrated," or write Temple Enterprises, 12007 Nebel Street, Rockville MD 20852; Stow-a-Way Foods, 166 Cushing Highway, Route 3A, Cohasset MA 02025; or Family Reserve Foods, 710 S.E. 17th St. Causeway, Fort Lauderdale FL 33316.

Eggs. Fresh eggs keep for months without refrigeration. Buy unrefrigerated eggs as fresh as possible and grease them with shortening or margarine. Store them in their cartons. Some sailors turn eggs weekly; I do not. Freeze-dried eggs, both cooked and raw, are available from camping suppliers. Dehydrated eggs are sold by reserve food stores, low-fat powdered eggs (Eggstra brand) are sold in the diet foods section of your supermarket, and pickled eggs are available in delicatessens.

Freeze-dried foods. Shop locally at camping supply stores, or write the firms listed under "Dehydrated foods" here. Request a free catalogue from REI Co-op, 1525 11th Avenue, Seattle WA 98122.

Fruit, candied. If you keep the container tightly lidded, and in the coolest spot possible, candied fruit will keep for months.

Fruit, dried. Commercial raisins, prunes, and other dried fruits keep for months, and their keeping qualities are generally excellent. Dehydrated canned fruits are available through reserve food outlets (check the Yellow Pages under Foods–Dehydrated), but dehydrates are drier and harder than packaged raisins and will require soaking or cooking.

Garlic. Buy fresh, well-dried whole garlic and allow good air circulation. Peel as needed.

Ham. Available canned, freeze-dried, imitation dehydrated, and country-cured. Country-cured hams are desirable because you cut off only as much as needed; wrap it loosely in cloth and scrape off mold as necessary. Sliced country ham in cellophane vacuum packs will keep for some time, but its keeping qualities are not as good as whole or half country hams. Country-cured hams, needing no refrigeration, are available from: Aunt Lucy Hams, Box 126, 3 Frederick St., Walkersville MD 21793; Beckton Farm Company, 3055 Medlin, Raleigh NC 27607; Harrington's, Richmond VT 05477; Hudson Ham House, Rt. 3 Box 27, Culpepper VA 22701; Joyner Smithfield Hams, Box 387, Smithfield VA 23430; McArthur's Smokehouse, Millerton NY 12546; Pepperidge Farm, Box 7000, Norwalk CT 06856. Such hams and bacons are sold in supermarkets in some areas, particularly in the southeastern United States.

Honey. Keeps indefinitely without refrigeration.

Jelly, jam. Opened jars will keep a couple of weeks without refrigeration, but use as quickly as possible. Buy small sizes and open only one at a time.

Ketchup. Keeps several weeks without refrigeration.

Lemons, limes. Buy fresh fruit in season. Allow good air circulation and avoid bruising. Pick the fruit over regularly to remove spoiled pieces. If the fruit dries out, soak it in hot water and then squeeze. Bottled juice keeps several weeks after opening if it's the type with a preservative added. Lemon is also available in crystal form, but it is highly hygroscopic.

Marshmallows. Double wrap and keep dry. Marshmallows will keep several months unless they get damp. Marshmallow cream (in jars) is also a good keeper and is handy to use on desserts and in cocoa.

Mayonnaise. See Chapter 11, "Stow-Aboard Salads," for salad dressings to make fresh. Keeping opened mayonnaise unrefrigerated is not recommended. Yogurt makes a good substitute in some recipes.

Milk. The most commonly available forms of milk, aside from fresh, are evaporated milk and nonfat dry milk. Canned whole milk is sold in some areas, along with canned cream, sour cream, and other dairy specialties. Most U.S. supermarkets now carry a dry milk that has some butterfat content, and in many other countries you'll find a powdered milk with a high butterfat content. Long-life milk comes in cardboard

cartons in several sizes and types, and lasts for months without refrigeration. Some supermarkets carry instant buttermilk mix. Reserve food outlets (look in the Yellow Pages under Foods–Dehydrated) offer nonfat dry milk in enameled, long-life tins.

Mustard. Prepared mustard keeps for weeks without refrigeration.

Nuts. Available canned salted, canned raw, canned toasted, whole, and shelled. Keep all nuts as cool and dry as possible. After opening, tinned nuts can stale quickly, especially if they are salted. Older nuts develop a strong oily taste. For long-term storage, rely on vacuum-pack nuts in cans or jars.

Onions. Buy firm, well-dried onions and allow them good air circulation. Keep them unbruised and dry. Yellow onions are good for cooking; red and yellow mild onions are good raw. Onions are an important staple when you are living on canned and packaged foods, so buy them generously. Onion is also available dried, and this will last well if kept very dry. There is bottled onion juice, powdered onion, and onion salt. Occasionally you can find dried salad onion flakes on supermarket shelves.

Oranges. Buy firm, fresh oranges and wrap them individually in paper toweling or brown paper. Pick them over occasionally and throw bad ones away. Oranges bought at their prime will last a couple of months aboard. Orange sections and mandarin oranges come in cans.

Orange juice. Available canned, and imitation orange drinks can be bought powdered in jars, packets, and tins.

Peanut butter. Keeps for months without refrigeration. Reserve food outlets carry powdered peanut butter in long-life tins.

Pickles. Most types will keep a week or more after opening, but open only one jar at a time, of course.

Potatoes. Buy firm, fresh potatoes in season, allow them good air circulation, keep them cool and dry, and pick off shoots as they develop. Examine potatoes regularly and discard any that begin to water or develop soft spots. Dried potatoes are available in cans and packages, and you can buy canned whole or sliced potatoes, canned potato sticks, or canned potato salads.

Relish. Most types will keep a week or far longer after opening. Open one variety at a time and use it quickly.

Salami, sausage, pepperoni. One clue to buying hard sausages is how they are stored by the supermarket. Look for types which are not kept refrigerated. Allow them good air circulation and keep them away from heat. Various sausages are also available canned and freeze-dried.

Sour cream. You'll find instant sour cream mix in packets at supermarkets and in cans at reserve food suppliers. You can use yogurt as a substitute for sour cream in many instances, or you can make a substitute by souring canned cream or evaporated milk with a little vinegar or lemon juice.

Squash. Look for varieties such as acorn and butternut that are traditionally kept over the winter. Buy them generously when they are in season, protect them from bruising, and provide good air circulation. Examine the stored squash every week or so, and use any that develop bad spots. Other squash varieties are available canned.

Sweet potato. Buy firm, fresh, unbruised sweet potatoes or yams. Keep them from bruising and allow them good air circulation. Sweet potato is also sold canned, dehydrated in cans, and, occasionally, in supermarkets in dried form.

Tomatoes. Buy farm-fresh (not cold-storage) tomatoes in green, pink, and red. Unripe tomatoes will continue to ripen, providing you with red tomatoes for many weeks.

Yeast. Available in dated packets, bulk cans in some supermarkets, and in long-life tins. See the sourdough section of Chapter 9, "Breads," for instructions on making and keeping your own yeast culture.

Yogurt. You may have noticed that many of the recipes in this book call for yogurt, but that doesn't mean a daily trip to the deli. Yogurt is a culture that you can keep going indefinitely on your boat, with careful management. Making yogurt on a boat brings about some special problems. For one thing, yogurt likes to be still while it "yogs" so yours just might not flourish in a rolly anchorage. It is also very choosy about temperature so you'll need a warm place (about 100°F.) for it to stand overnight. Yet you'll kill it with milk that is too hot. Although I've made yogurt using only a very heavy, lidded saucepan wrapped in a thick towel, it's best to use a wide-mouth vacuum bottle to maintain an even temperature while the organisms do their thing.

To start your yogurt, either buy the commercial product, preferably a natural type, or a dried yogurt starter from a health-food store. (They can be ordered from Walnut Acres, Penns Creek PA 17862.) Although most home recipes call for making yogurt with whole or skim milk, I prefer using nonfat dry milk. It doesn't contain the enzyme that fresh milk does, one which requires that milk be scalded and then cooled before making yogurt or yeast products. Also, you can add more dry milk to make your yogurt extra thick and creamy.

Simply fill a container one-third to half full with nonfat dry milk, fill with pleasantly warm water (about 100°), and add a tablespoon of yogurt from your last batch. (There is no need to add more. In fact, adding too much starter may crowd the bacilli, giving you a thin and watery result.) Let it stand overnight in a still, warm place. By morning you'll have yogurt to eat and use in recipes. The next night, repeat the procedure.

If you can refrigerate the yogurt it will keep for a week or more for use as a starter, but unrefrigerated, the organism soon devours its available food, which must be renewed. Keep the ball rolling by using yogurt in all the usual ways, as well as substituting it for mayonnaise, sour milk, and sour cream in recipes. You'll have no problem using at least a small batch a day.

Still, it's best to carry several extra packets of starter. You may tire of the nightly culturing routine, or your yogurt may develop unpleasant colors or tastes if undesirable organisms in the air begin growing in the culture. During long passages, your culture may not survive the constant movement.

Despite the problems of keeping it alive, yogurt is a nourishing, versatile food which can be made fresh as you go.

Note: while all the foods listed here will keep for some time without refrigeration, some common-sense cooperation is needed. Mold spores are everywhere, so foods like jelly and relish will naturally mold faster if you leave them unlidded. It's best to dip into such foods with a clean spoon or knife. Each time you use one which is not clean, you are introducing new bacteria which can start multiplying. You should also keep all food items away from excessive heat; avoid lockers next to the engine room, lockers directly under a dark-colored deck, and any stowage spots where direct sun can hit the food through a port.

INDEX